Table of Contents

Introduction **6**
The Global Impact of Silver and Grey Icons 6
International Triumphs and Worldwide Recognition 10
A Glimpse into the Global Racing Stage 14
Chapter 1: Winx (Australia, 2011-2019), Bay (appeared greyish in some light) **18**
Winx's early races and ascent to stardom 18
Her Unprecedented 33-Race Win Streak and Multiple Cox Plate Victories 23
The Historic Queen Elizabeth Stakes Victory 27
Her Legacy as an Australian and Global Racing Legend .. 31
Chapter 2: Dancing Brave (United Kingdom, 1983-1999), Grey **35**
Dancing Brave's Origins and Promising Early Career 35
The Remarkable 1986 Prix de l'Arc de Triomphe Victory .. 39
His Enduring Status as a Champion 43
The Impact of Dancing Brave on the International Stage . 47
Chapter 3: Zenyatta (United States, 2004-2020), Bay (appeared greyish in some light) **51**
Zenyatta's Journey from Early Races to Becoming an Icon 51
Her Unbeaten Streak and Breeders' Cup Classic Victory ... 55
The Global Recognition of a Beloved American Mare 59

The Legacy of Zenyatta in the Hearts of Fans 63

Chapter 4: Nashwan (United Kingdom, 1986-2002), Grey **67**

Nashwan's Early Career and the Path to Becoming a Champion 67

His 1989 Epsom Derby Victory and 2000 Guineas Triumph 71

The International Recognition of Nashwan's Greatness 75

His Enduring Presence in the History of Horse Racing 79

Chapter 5: Global Triumphs Unveiled **83**

Exploring the Global Feats of These Iconic Racehorses 83

The Impact of Their International Success and Recognition 86

The Unique Qualities That Set Them Apart on the Global Stage 90

Chapter 6: The World's Jockeys: Partners in Glory **94**

Recognizing the Jockeys Who Played Crucial Roles in These Horses' International Triumphs 94

The Connections and International Collaborations That Contributed to Their Success 98

The Challenges and Triumphs Faced by Horse and Rider Across Different Nations 102

Chapter 7: A Global Legacy Beyond Borders **106**

Copyright © 2023 by William R. Foster (Author)

All rights reserved. No part of this book may be reproduced or utilized in any form or by any means, electronic or mechanical, including photocopying, recording or by any information storage and retrieval system, without permission in writing from the publisher, except for brief quotations in critical articles or reviews.

The content of this book is based on various sources and is intended for educational and entertainment purposes only. While the author has made every effort to ensure the accuracy, completeness, and reliability of the information provided, the information may be subject to errors, omissions, or inaccuracies. Therefore, the author makes no warranties, express or implied, regarding the content of this book.

Readers are advised to seek the guidance of a licensed professional before attempting any techniques or actions outlined in this book. The author is not responsible for any losses, damages, or injuries that may arise from the use of information contained within. The information provided in this book is not intended to be a substitute for professional advice, and readers should not rely solely on the information presented.

By reading this book, readers acknowledge that the author is not providing legal, financial, medical, or professional advice. Any reliance on the information contained in this book is solely at the reader's own risk.

Thank you for selecting this book as a valuable source of knowledge and inspiration. Our aim is to provide you with insights and information that will enrich your understanding and enhance your personal growth. We appreciate your decision to embark on this journey of discovery with us, and we hope that this book will exceed your expectations and leave a lasting impact on your life.

Title: Whispers of Mist and Triumph: Global Feats Unforgotten
Subtitle: Triumphs of International Racing Icons

Series: Tales of the Turf: The Legacy of White and Grey
Author: William R. Foster

Celebrating the Records, Achievements, and Impact of These International Icons *106*
The Enduring Fascination and Love for 'Whispers of Mist and Triumph' *110*
The Global Racing Community's Connection to These Unforgettable Champions *113*
Conclusion **116**
The Global Influence of White and Grey Icons *116*
International Success and the Worldwide Racing Community *120*
A Tribute to Global Legends of the Turf *124*
Wordbook **127**
Supplementary Materials **130**

Introduction

The Global Impact of Silver and Grey Icons

Horse racing is a sport that transcends borders and cultures, a testament to the enduring connection between humans and these magnificent animals. While every racehorse carries a unique story, our journey begins with those whose coats shimmered with silver and grey, an ethereal presence on the track. In this introductory chapter, we delve into the world of iconic white and grey-coated racehorses, exploring the profound impact they've had on the international stage.

The Allure of White and Grey

The gleaming white and majestic grey coats of racehorses have long held a fascination for enthusiasts and novices alike. These horses, appearing as if wrapped in the mist of their own legends, have captured the imaginations of generations. They stand out not only for their beauty but also for their remarkable abilities on the racetrack.

A World of Achievements

This chapter pays tribute to the equine heroes that have graced the tracks around the world. From the rolling hills of the United Kingdom to the sunburnt plains of Australia, from the lush pastures of the United States to the historic tracks of France, these horses transcended geographic boundaries. With speed, endurance, and the heart of champions, they showcased their prowess, leaving an indelible mark on the global racing community.

A Glimpse into the Remarkable Stories

We will begin our journey with Winx, an Australian wonder whose greyish appearance in certain lights only added to her mystique. Winx's story is one of unwavering dominance, her 33-race win streak standing as a testament to her unparalleled talent. In Chapter 1, we will explore her early races, her ascent to stardom, and the historic victories that made her an Australian and global legend.

Chapter 2 is dedicated to Dancing Brave, the grey-coated champion from the United Kingdom. His victory in the 1986 Prix de l'Arc de Triomphe is still remembered as one of the greatest moments in racing history. We'll delve into his origins, promising early career, and his lasting legacy on the international stage.

Zenyatta, the American mare with a coat that seemed to shimmer with hints of grey, takes center stage in Chapter 3. Her unbeaten streak and Breeders' Cup Classic victory captivated audiences not only in the United States but around the world. We'll trace her journey from early races to icon status and explore her lasting legacy in the hearts of fans.

Nashwan, the grey-coated sensation from the United Kingdom, comes into focus in Chapter 4. We'll unravel his early career, the path to becoming a champion, and the international recognition of his greatness. His victories in the 1989 Epsom Derby and the 2000 Guineas cemented his place in history.

The Unforgettable Impact

These remarkable stories are more than mere records; they are chapters in the history of horse racing. Each of these iconic horses is a testament to the passion and dedication of all those involved in the sport – the trainers, breeders, owners, and, of course, the jockeys. We will delve into the international collaborations and challenges faced by horse and rider across different nations in Chapter 6, "The World's Jockeys: Partners in Glory."

As we explore these stories, we will uncover the unique qualities that set these horses apart on the global stage in Chapter 5, "Global Triumphs Unveiled." Their feats are not just wins; they are a testament to the human spirit's unwavering dedication to the pursuit of excellence.

A Global Connection

The stories of these white and grey icons extend beyond the racetrack. They have become a part of the collective memory of the global racing community. In

Chapter 7, "A Global Legacy Beyond Borders," we celebrate the records, achievements, and lasting impact of these international icons. Their legacy is a testament to the enduring fascination and love for 'Whispers of Mist and Triumph.'

This introductory chapter sets the stage for a journey through the lives and achievements of these remarkable horses and the profound connections they forged across borders. As we delve into their individual stories, we will uncover the threads that weave together the tapestry of international horse racing, where these white and grey icons will forever be celebrated.

International Triumphs and Worldwide Recognition

Horse racing, a sport with roots stretching across centuries and continents, has always been a tapestry of global competition and shared admiration for the equine athletes who grace its tracks. While the world of horse racing is teeming with extraordinary stories of triumph and perseverance, this chapter delves into the international triumphs and worldwide recognition earned by the silver and grey icons, those ethereal champions whose elegance and speed know no borders.

The Global Stage

Horse racing is a global spectacle, with each region contributing its unique flavor and champions to the grand tapestry of the sport. It is on this grand stage that the silver and grey icons have left an indelible mark, thrilling audiences worldwide.

Winx: The Australian Wonder

Winx, the bay mare who occasionally appeared greyish in certain light, captured not only the hearts of Australians but also the admiration of horse racing enthusiasts around the globe. In Chapter 1, we explored her journey from humble beginnings to her ascent to stardom. Now, let us dive deeper into her international triumphs.

The Australian turf became Winx's kingdom, but her dominion extended far beyond. Her unprecedented 33-race win streak, a feat that has no parallel in modern racing, is a testament to her extraordinary abilities. Among her numerous conquests, her victories in the Cox Plate stand as a pinnacle in the sport. These achievements resonated not only with the Australian audience but also with fans from diverse corners of the world, proving that greatness knows no borders.

Dancing Brave: The United Kingdom's Champion

Dancing Brave, the grey-coated sensation from the United Kingdom, wasn't just a national treasure; he was an international sensation. In Chapter 2, we explored his promising early career and his historic 1986 Prix de l'Arc de Triomphe victory. Now, let's unravel the magnitude of his global recognition.

The Prix de l'Arc de Triomphe is one of the most prestigious races in the world, drawing the finest thoroughbreds from across the globe. Dancing Brave's triumph in this iconic event was a defining moment in the history of horse racing, and it reverberated through international racing circles. His legacy as a champion stretched beyond borders, inspiring admiration and respect on a global scale.

Zenyatta: The Beloved American Mare

In Chapter 3, we explored the journey of Zenyatta, the American bay mare whose greyish hints added to her mystique. Her unbeaten streak and Breeders' Cup Classic victory secured her a special place in the hearts of American fans. Now, we uncover her international recognition.

Zenyatta's achievements went beyond her unbeaten streak. They represented a symbol of hope and inspiration for an entire nation. Her presence at the Breeders' Cup Classic transcended horse racing; it became a moment of unity and shared celebration. International observers couldn't help but be drawn to her remarkable performances, marking her as a beloved figure worldwide.

Nashwan: The United Kingdom's Grey Sensation

Chapter 4 introduced us to Nashwan, the grey-coated sensation from the United Kingdom, and his early career, culminating in victories at the Epsom Derby and the 2000 Guineas. Now, we explore his international recognition.

Nashwan's triumphs in these iconic British races echoed throughout the international racing community. The Epsom Derby, in particular, has a storied history and global significance, and Nashwan's victory cemented his place as a champion not only in the United Kingdom but also in the hearts of racing enthusiasts around the world.

The Global Impact of Silver and Grey Icons

The international recognition of these silver and grey icons is a testament to the global appeal of horse racing. It is a sport where borders blur, and the spirit of competition and admiration for these equine marvels unites fans worldwide. As we journey through the lives and triumphs of these iconic horses, we will continue to uncover the depth of their international impact. These remarkable horses are not confined to one nation or one era; they belong to the world, leaving behind a legacy that transcends borders and endures through time.

In the following chapters, we will delve deeper into the specifics of each horse's journey and the unique qualities that set them apart on the global stage. We will celebrate not only their victories but the connections they forged with fans and fellow enthusiasts worldwide. These horses have become the embodiment of international sportsmanship and the enduring spirit of the global horse racing community.

A Glimpse into the Global Racing Stage

To understand the profound impact of silver and grey icons on the world of horse racing, we must first step onto the global racing stage, a vibrant arena where cultures, traditions, and the spirit of competition converge. In this section, we take a closer look at the international landscape of horse racing, setting the scene for the remarkable stories of these equine champions whose silver and grey coats shimmered under the spotlight of worldwide recognition.

The Global Tapestry of Horse Racing

Horse racing is a sport woven into the very fabric of human history. Its origins can be traced back to ancient civilizations, from the chariot races of the Roman Empire to the steppes of Mongolia where Genghis Khan's cavalry showcased their equine prowess. Today, horse racing thrives as a global sport, connecting people from diverse backgrounds in a shared passion for speed, elegance, and competition.

The United Kingdom: Birthplace of Modern Racing

Our journey begins in the United Kingdom, often referred to as the "Home of Horse Racing." The lush meadows of Newmarket, the historic stands of Epsom Downs, and the prestigious Royal Ascot are synonymous with the sport's heritage. In the heart of this island nation, generations of horse racing enthusiasts have witnessed the birth of legends, including Dancing Brave, one of the silver and grey icons we celebrate in this book.

Australia: The Land of Legends

Down under, Australia boasts a racing culture deeply ingrained in its history. The thundering hooves of thoroughbreds have resonated across the vast expanse of the Australian outback. The country has produced some of the most remarkable horses in the history of the sport, and one such legend is Winx. Her dominance on Australian tracks and her international acclaim make her a symbol of pride for a nation passionate about racing.

The United States: Where Dreams Gallop

In the United States, the sport of horse racing thrives on diversity and dreams. From the iconic Churchill Downs to the sweeping greens of Santa Anita Park, the American racing landscape is as varied as the nation itself. Zenyatta, the beloved bay mare with greyish hints, left an indelible mark in the hearts of American racing fans. Her journey from humble beginnings to a global icon reflects the American spirit of perseverance and excellence.

France: A Hub of Prestige

France, with its rich racing history, showcases a unique blend of tradition and innovation. The Prix de l'Arc de Triomphe, often regarded as the world's premier middle-distance horse race, is a testament to the country's commitment to the sport. Dancing Brave's triumph in this race elevated him to international stardom, and his story exemplifies the prestige of French racing.

A Global Audience

Horse racing is no longer confined to the borders of a single nation. It is a global spectacle that captures the imagination of fans from every corner of the world. Thanks to modern communication and technology, races are beamed into living rooms, smartphones, and tablets, allowing fans to witness the exploits of their equine heroes from the farthest reaches of the planet.

International Racing Festivals

Throughout the year, the racing world converges at international festivals that transcend boundaries. Events like the Dubai World Cup, the Hong Kong International Races, and the Breeders' Cup World Championships serve as platforms where the best horses from different regions come together in a symphony of competition. These events provide the stage where the silver and grey icons showcased their prowess and made a lasting impact.

A World of Possibilities

The global stage of horse racing is a world of possibilities, where dreams are born, records are shattered, and the spirit of competition binds people from diverse cultures. As we embark on a journey through the lives and achievements of these remarkable racehorses, it's crucial to remember that they weren't just local heroes; they were global sensations. Their stories resonate with anyone who has ever felt the exhilaration of a horse race, regardless of their location or background.

In the following chapters, we will delve deeper into the individual stories of these silver and grey icons, exploring their journeys from local tracks to international stardom. We will witness their triumphs and the lasting impact they left on the world of horse racing, demonstrating that excellence in this sport knows no boundaries.

Chapter 1: Winx (Australia, 2011-2019), Bay (appeared greyish in some light)

Winx's early races and ascent to stardom

In the heart of the Australian racing landscape, a legend was born. Winx, the bay mare whose coat occasionally shimmered with a hint of grey, left an indelible mark on the world of horse racing. Her remarkable journey from humble beginnings to international stardom is a tale of talent, perseverance, and the unwavering spirit that defines champions.

A Humble Beginning

Winx's story begins in the lush pastures of the Hunter Valley, Australia, where she was foaled in 2011. Bred by Fairway Thoroughbreds, she came into the world with the blood of champions coursing through her veins. Her sire, Street Cry, and dam, Vegas Showgirl, set the stage for a remarkable lineage. But the path to greatness is often paved with challenges, and Winx's early days were no exception.

As a yearling, Winx was not an imposing figure. Her unassuming appearance belied the power and grace she would later exhibit on the track. In the competitive world of thoroughbred racing, where yearlings are evaluated with a critical eye, she had to prove herself worthy of attention.

The Influence of Trainer Chris Waller

It was under the guidance of trainer Chris Waller that Winx's potential began to emerge. Waller, a respected figure in Australian racing, recognized something special in the unassuming filly. His patience and expertise were instrumental in shaping Winx into the champion she would become.

Waller's training methods, honed through years of experience, allowed Winx to develop at her own pace. Her early races were stepping stones, opportunities to learn and grow. Each outing on the track was a chance for Winx to refine her racing skills and demonstrate her potential.

The Early Races

Winx's early races were marked by promise and flashes of brilliance. Although she had yet to achieve the commanding dominance that would later define her, those who watched her closely could see the glimmers of greatness. Her maiden win at Warwick Farm in June 2014 hinted at her potential, and her performances in the Group races demonstrated her ability to compete at a higher level.

In this chapter, we will delve into these early races, exploring the victories and lessons that paved the way for her ascent to stardom. We will relive the moments when her latent talent began to unfurl, captivating the imagination of racing enthusiasts across Australia and beyond.

Rise to Stardom

The turning point in Winx's career came with her victory in the Group 1 Queensland Oaks. This win marked her emergence as a force to be reckoned with in Australian racing. From this point forward, her ascent to stardom was nothing short of meteoric.

As her winning streak continued, with race after race falling to her mastery, Winx captured the hearts of a nation. Her performances transcended the sport, turning her into a household name in Australia. Her charismatic jockey, Hugh Bowman, formed an unbreakable partnership with the mare, and together they achieved the extraordinary.

The Unprecedented 33-Race Win Streak

Perhaps the most iconic chapter in Winx's story is her unprecedented 33-race win streak. In the world of horse racing, where defeat is a constant companion, her consistency and sheer dominance were awe-inspiring. The records she shattered, the challenges she overcame, and the fervor she inspired among fans make this win streak a remarkable achievement in the history of the sport.

Multiple Cox Plate Victories

The Cox Plate is one of the most prestigious races in Australia, and it became Winx's stage for greatness. Her victories in the Cox Plate not only added to her legend but also solidified her status as a national treasure. Each win in this iconic race added a new layer to the narrative of her career.

The Historic Queen Elizabeth Stakes Victory

Winx's international acclaim reached new heights when she ventured beyond Australian shores to compete in the Queen Elizabeth Stakes. Her victory in this race was not only a testament to her versatility but also a demonstration of her ability to excel on the global stage. It was a moment that showcased her as a horse of exceptional talent and enduring appeal.

Legacy as an Australian and Global Racing Legend

As we explore Winx's early races and her remarkable ascent to stardom, we will uncover the qualities that made her a racing phenomenon. Her story is not just a tale of victories; it is a testament to the potential that lies within every racehorse and the indomitable spirit that sets champions apart.

Winx's legacy is not confined to the records she shattered; it lives on in the hearts of racing enthusiasts and serves as an inspiration to all who dream of achieving greatness in the world of horse racing. Her journey is a reminder that champions are not born; they are made through dedication, perseverance, and an unwavering belief in the pursuit of excellence.

Her Unprecedented 33-Race Win Streak and Multiple Cox Plate Victories

In the annals of horse racing, there are moments that stand as monuments to greatness, and there are achievements that seem to defy the very laws of the sport. Winx's unprecedented 33-race win streak and her multiple victories in the coveted Cox Plate are such moments, etched in history as an awe-inspiring testament to her brilliance.

A Streak Like No Other

When Winx stepped onto the racetrack, there was an aura of invincibility about her. Her impressive early races had hinted at her potential, but it was the beginning of a streak that would leave the racing world in awe.

The win streak started in earnest in May 2015 when she crossed the line first at Rosehill Gardens. From that point on, Winx's journey became a relentless march toward history. Each race, each victory, was a step closer to the extraordinary.

As the numbers mounted, her name became synonymous with the notion of invulnerability. The racing community watched in rapt attention as she bested one challenger after another. The Australian turf was hers, and she defended her dominion with unwavering determination.

The Challenge of Consistency

In the world of horse racing, where unforeseen variables can derail even the best-laid plans, sustaining a win streak is an exceptional feat. It's a testament not only to the horse's abilities but also to the skill of her trainer, Chris Waller, and the synergy between jockey and mare.

Hugh Bowman, Winx's regular jockey, became an integral part of her success. His partnership with the mare was characterized by an innate understanding of her abilities and the ability to bring out the best in her. Their collaboration was a key factor in maintaining the extraordinary win streak.

The Hurdles and the Triumphs

Over the course of the 33-race win streak, Winx faced a myriad of challenges. From wet tracks to firm surfaces, from shorter sprints to extended distances, she displayed her versatility and adaptability. Each challenge was met with composure and class, and it was this ability to perform under a variety of conditions that set her apart.

One of the notable aspects of her win streak was the manner in which she continued to elevate her game. The races were not mere repetitions of past victories but showcases of her ever-improving form. The way she dispatched rivals in a race was a testament to her ability to learn, adapt, and excel.

The Cox Plate: A Stage of Greatness

The Cox Plate, known as the 'race where legends are made,' stands as one of the most prestigious events in Australian racing. It's a race that draws the finest thoroughbreds from around the world, and it became the ultimate stage for Winx to display her greatness.

Winx's victories in the Cox Plate are among the defining moments of her career. The first of her four wins in the race came in 2015, and she went on to create history by becoming the only horse to claim the Cox Plate four times consecutively. Each of these victories was a masterclass in racing, a demonstration of her ability to not only win but to do so in style.

The Race of the Century

Among her Cox Plate triumphs, the 2018 edition stands out as a remarkable chapter in her story. In what was billed as the 'Race of the Century,' Winx faced a formidable field that included the likes of Benbatl and Humidor. The world watched in anticipation as Winx and Hugh Bowman executed a stunning victory, further solidifying her status as a global racing sensation.

The Legacy of the Win Streak and Cox Plate Victories

As we delve into the saga of Winx's unprecedented 33-race win streak and her multiple Cox Plate victories, we find a narrative that transcends statistics and records. Her achievements are not just a list of numbers but a testament to the extraordinary potential of thoroughbred racing.

Winx's legacy is not confined to the records she shattered; it lives on in the hearts of racing enthusiasts, a reminder that in the pursuit of excellence, the limits of achievement are boundless. Her story is a testament to the dedication of all those involved in the sport, from the trainers to the jockeys, and the enduring spirit of a champion mare who left a mark on horse racing that will be cherished for generations to come.

The Historic Queen Elizabeth Stakes Victory

In the storied history of Australian horse racing, there are moments that transcend the sport, encapsulating the essence of greatness. Winx's victory in the Queen Elizabeth Stakes is one of those moments, a race that not only added a new chapter to her legend but also showcased her prowess on the international stage.

The Queen Elizabeth Stakes: A Prestigious Stage

The Queen Elizabeth Stakes, one of the most prestigious horse races in Australia, takes place at Sydney's Royal Randwick Racecourse. It stands as a testament to the nation's enduring love for the sport and is named in honor of Queen Elizabeth II, a symbol of the enduring connection between horse racing and the British monarchy.

The race, held over a distance of 2,020 meters, attracts the finest horses from around the world. It is a true test of a horse's abilities, requiring both speed and stamina. It's a race where champions are crowned, and legends are forged.

Winx's Debut in the Queen Elizabeth Stakes

By the time Winx made her debut in the Queen Elizabeth Stakes in 2017, she had already established herself as one of the greatest racehorses Australia had ever seen. Her unprecedented 17-race win streak had captured the hearts of a nation, and the anticipation for her appearance in the Queen Elizabeth Stakes was electrifying.

The 2017 Queen Elizabeth Stakes marked her first attempt at the race, and it was a momentous occasion for racing enthusiasts. The world watched with bated breath as Winx, under the guidance of jockey Hugh Bowman and the expert training of Chris Waller, prepared to take on a field of talented rivals.

A Triumph for the Ages

The 2017 Queen Elizabeth Stakes unfolded as an epic battle of the titans. Winx was pitted against a formidable field that included champion galloper Hartnell and the rising star Humidor. The race became a showcase of talent, a display of thoroughbred excellence that left spectators spellbound.

As the field thundered down the Royal Randwick straight, Winx, with her trademark explosive turn of foot, surged to the front. It was a defining moment, a display of her unparalleled ability to accelerate and leave her rivals in her wake. In a matter of seconds, she had created a lead that was insurmountable, and she crossed the finish line with a comfortable margin, securing her first Queen Elizabeth Stakes victory.

A Repeat Performance: The 2018 Queen Elizabeth Stakes

Winx's victory in the 2017 Queen Elizabeth Stakes was nothing short of magical. It was a moment when a champion mare had etched her name in the annals of the sport. However, she wasn't done.

The following year, in 2018, Winx returned to the Queen Elizabeth Stakes to defend her crown. Her victory in the previous edition had only heightened the expectations, and fans around the world eagerly anticipated her performance.

The 2018 Queen Elizabeth Stakes unfolded as a repeat performance of the previous year, with Winx once again demonstrating her sheer dominance. Her remarkable acceleration and ability to maintain her speed over the 2,020-meter distance left no doubt about her status as the world's best racehorse.

A Legacy Beyond Borders

Winx's victories in the Queen Elizabeth Stakes were not just remarkable for their excellence; they were symbolic of her ability to excel on the international stage. In a sport where champions are often defined by their performances beyond their home turf, Winx's success in the Queen

Elizabeth Stakes underscored her versatility and adaptability.

Her story is one of transcending boundaries, of showing that greatness knows no borders. The Queen Elizabeth Stakes victories stand as a testament to her impact not only on Australian racing but on the global racing community.

The Enduring Legacy

As we explore the historic Queen Elizabeth Stakes victories in Winx's career, we are reminded that her story is not just about wins and records. It's a narrative of inspiration, of the unrelenting pursuit of excellence, and of a mare whose legacy will endure for generations to come.

The Queen Elizabeth Stakes became a stage for Winx to showcase her unparalleled talent and to create moments that will forever be etched in the memory of racing enthusiasts. Her victories in the race are more than just statistics; they are a testament to the enduring spirit of a champion who defied expectations and redefined the limits of excellence.

Her Legacy as an Australian and Global Racing Legend

Winx, the bay mare with a hint of grey in certain light, transcended the confines of a racetrack to become an icon not only in Australia but on the international stage. Her legacy as a racing legend is a testament to her remarkable career and her enduring impact on the world of horse racing.

A Nation's Beloved Champion

In the heart of Australia, Winx captured the imagination and hearts of a nation. Her unprecedented 33-race win streak was more than just a sporting achievement; it was a source of national pride. Australians from all walks of life rallied around her, making her a beloved figure in a country where horse racing is more than a pastime; it's a part of the nation's cultural fabric.

From the bustling city of Sydney to the vast expanses of the Australian outback, Winx's name resonated. The sound of her thundering hooves created an indomitable rhythm that reverberated across the land. Her appearances at racetracks were events in themselves, drawing crowds of fans who came not just to witness her victories but to be part of a historic moment.

The Magic of the Mile

One of Winx's most remarkable attributes was her ability to excel over a range of distances. Her performances in mile races, particularly in the Group 1 Doncaster Handicap, were a testament to her versatility. Her victories in the Doncaster showcased her as a horse who could produce an electrifying turn of foot, leaving her rivals in awe.

The magic of the mile races extended to her international appearances, where she demonstrated her adaptability. Her ability to excel in different conditions and distances made her a truly global sensation.

Transcending Borders: International Acclaim

Winx's journey to international recognition was not limited to the borders of Australia. Her appearances on the global stage, such as her victories in the Queen Elizabeth Stakes, demonstrated her ability to compete against the best horses from around the world.

The global racing community watched with admiration as Winx showcased her talent beyond Australian shores. Her victories in prestigious international races added another layer to her legacy, establishing her as a horse who could excel on the world stage.

The Connection with the Fans

Winx's connection with her fans, often referred to as 'Winx Nation,' was one of the most endearing aspects of her career. Her charisma extended beyond her victories on the racetrack; it encompassed her interactions with the people who adored her.

The mare's accessibility endeared her to racing enthusiasts. Fans could visit her in her stable, attend trackwork sessions, and witness her preparation for races. This level of accessibility was unprecedented for a horse of her caliber, and it further solidified her place in the hearts of her admirers.

The Legacy Continues

As Winx's career came to a close in 2019, the question of her legacy arose. What would be the enduring impact of a horse who had rewritten the history books? The answer became clear in the months and years that followed.

Her legacy is not confined to the racetrack; it lives on in the breeding barn, where her descendants carry the torch of her lineage. Her legacy lives in the hearts of racing enthusiasts who will forever remember her as the horse of a lifetime. Her legacy lives in the countless photographs, memorabilia, and stories that celebrate her remarkable journey.

The Winx Effect

The 'Winx Effect' became a term used to describe the phenomenon she created. It was a sense of anticipation, a belief that greatness could be witnessed with every race. Her legacy is a reminder that horse racing is not just about statistics and records; it's about the moments that define the sport.

Winx's story is a testament to the enduring spirit of a champion. Her legacy is not just Australian; it's global. Her name is spoken with reverence in racing circles around the world, and her impact continues to be felt in the hearts of those who have been touched by her extraordinary career.

As we explore Winx's legacy as an Australian and global racing legend, we come to understand that her impact goes beyond the sport. She represents the embodiment of excellence, the pursuit of perfection, and the enduring connection between horses and humanity. She is not just a champion; she is an inspiration, a symbol of what can be achieved when talent, dedication, and the unwavering spirit of a champion come together in perfect harmony.

Chapter 2: Dancing Brave (United Kingdom, 1983-1999), Grey

Dancing Brave's Origins and Promising Early Career

In the world of horse racing, legends are often born from humble beginnings, and Dancing Brave, the magnificent grey from the United Kingdom, was no exception. His journey from birth to his early racing career is a tale of promise and potential, setting the stage for a legacy that would resonate through the ages.

A Star is Born

Dancing Brave, foaled in 1983, entered the world at Woodditton Stud in Newmarket, a place steeped in racing tradition. Bred by Khalid Abdullah, a prominent figure in the world of thoroughbred racing, the young colt's pedigree hinted at greatness. His sire, Lyphard, and dam, Navajo Princess, were both renowned in their own right, and the combination of their bloodlines ignited the spark of potential in the grey foal.

From the moment he took his first wobbly steps, there was something captivating about Dancing Brave. His distinctive grey coat set him apart, but it was his presence and the way he carried himself that hinted at the champion he would become. As he grew, his physical attributes only added to his allure. With a strong, elegant build and a distinctive star on his forehead, he was a horse destined to captivate the racing world.

The Early Days of Training

Dancing Brave's early training was entrusted to Guy Harwood, a respected figure in British racing. Under Harwood's watchful eye, the young colt began to hone his natural talents. His early workouts were a revelation, as he displayed an effortless stride and an innate understanding of the racetrack.

One of the aspects that set Dancing Brave apart was his composure. Even as a young horse, he exuded a sense of calm and control that is rare in the world of racing. It was as if he knew he was destined for greatness and was patiently waiting for his moment to shine.

The Unveiling: Debut Races

Dancing Brave made his racing debut in 1985 at Goodwood, and it was a moment that racing enthusiasts would come to cherish. The young colt, still learning the ropes of the sport, announced his arrival with a victory that hinted at the potential he carried. It was the beginning of a journey that would take him to the pinnacle of horse racing.

His early races were marked by promise. As he continued to gain experience, it became clear that Dancing Brave possessed a remarkable turn of foot. His ability to accelerate and leave his rivals behind was a harbinger of the dominance he would later achieve.

The Classic Year: 1986

In 1986, Dancing Brave's star rose to unprecedented heights. It was the year when he would capture the imagination of racing enthusiasts with performances that bordered on the ethereal. The colt's campaign included classic races, and it was in these marquee events that he would etch his name in the annals of history.

The 2000 Guineas

The 2000 Guineas, a classic race for three-year-olds, is one of the most prestigious events in British racing. Dancing Brave's performance in this race was nothing short of spectacular. With the jockeying skills of Greville Starkey, he produced a remarkable turn of foot that left his rivals trailing. It was a performance that elevated him to a new level of stardom.

The Epsom Derby

The Epsom Derby is often regarded as the ultimate test of a racehorse's abilities. It's a race where champions are separated from contenders, and Dancing Brave's victory in the 1986 edition was a demonstration of his exceptional talent. His acceleration on the iconic Epsom Downs left a lasting impression, and it was a moment that defined his legacy.

A Legacy Begins

Dancing Brave's origins and promising early career laid the foundation for a legacy that would endure through the ages. His rise from a grey foal in Newmarket to a classic-winning champion was a story that captured the hearts of racing enthusiasts not only in the United Kingdom but around the world.

As we delve into the early days of Dancing Brave, we uncover the qualities that set him apart, the promise he held, and the impact he would have on the global racing stage. His story is a reminder that champions are not solely defined by their victories but by the journey they undertake, the potential they carry, and the legacy they leave behind.

The Remarkable 1986 Prix de l'Arc de Triomphe Victory

In the world of thoroughbred horse racing, few events hold the prestige and significance of the Prix de l'Arc de Triomphe. Dancing Brave's victory in the 1986 edition of this iconic race marked a moment of history anchad is often regarded as one of the most remarkable performances in the sport.

The Arc: A Race of Distinction

The Prix de l'Arc de Triomphe, commonly referred to as "the Arc," is a race that transcends boundaries. Held annually at Longchamp Racecourse in Paris, France, it is considered one of the most prestigious turf races in the world. The race draws the finest horses from around the globe, each vying for the title of the best middle-distance horse.

Dancing Brave's Arrival in France

In the lead-up to the 1986 Arc, Dancing Brave's reputation had already crossed borders. The British colt had gained recognition as a horse of exceptional talent, and the racing world was eager to witness his performance on the grand stage of Longchamp.

Trained by Guy Harwood and ridden by Greville Starkey, Dancing Brave arrived in France with an air of anticipation. His appearances in the lead-up races had only added to the sense of excitement, as he displayed his characteristic turn of foot and an effortless stride that had already left racing enthusiasts in awe.

The Unfolding Drama

The 1986 Prix de l'Arc de Triomphe had all the makings of a classic showdown. It was a race that pitted Dancing Brave against some of the finest horses in the world, including Bering, Triptych, and Shahrastani. The field was a constellation of talent, and the world watched in anticipation.

As the race began, it quickly became evident that Dancing Brave was in a league of his own. The horse's ability to accelerate on the soft Longchamp turf was nothing short of extraordinary. He surged ahead, leaving his rivals struggling to catch up. Greville Starkey's skills as a jockey, coupled with Dancing Brave's remarkable turn of foot, were on full display.

The Arc: A Dominant Victory

As Dancing Brave powered down the Longchamp straight, it was clear that this was a performance for the ages. He not only won the Prix de l'Arc de Triomphe but did so in record-breaking fashion. His victory margin was substantial, and his time of completion remains one of the fastest in the history of the race.

The manner in which Dancing Brave left his rivals behind was a spectacle that captured the imagination of racing enthusiasts. It was not just a win; it was a display of sheer dominance, a moment when a horse transcended the ordinary to become something truly extraordinary.

A Global Impact

Dancing Brave's victory in the 1986 Prix de l'Arc de Triomphe was not just a British triumph; it was a global moment. His performance was a testament to the unifying power of horse racing, where individuals from different nations could come together to appreciate the sheer brilliance of a thoroughbred.

The victory extended Dancing Brave's reputation as one of the finest racehorses in the world. His legacy as a champion was no longer confined to the United Kingdom; it had become an international story, a narrative of excellence that transcended borders.

The Enduring Legacy of the Arc

The 1986 Prix de l'Arc de Triomphe victory marked a high point in Dancing Brave's career, but it also set the stage for a legacy that would endure for generations. The race became a symbol of his exceptional talent, a reference point when discussing the greatest middle-distance horses in history.

Dancing Brave's performance in the Arc is remembered not just for the victory but for the manner in which it was achieved. It is a reminder that the sport of horse racing is not just about wins and losses; it's about moments of brilliance, of horses and jockeys coming together in perfect harmony to create magic on the racetrack.

As we explore Dancing Brave's remarkable victory in the 1986 Prix de l'Arc de Triomphe, we delve into a chapter of racing history that remains etched in the memory of enthusiasts. It is a story of a horse who, on a cool day in Longchamp, showed the world what it means to be a champion.

His Enduring Status as a Champion

Dancing Brave's legacy is not just a collection of statistics and race victories; it's a testament to his enduring status as a champion. His remarkable career left an indelible mark on the world of horse racing, and his name continues to evoke admiration and reverence, decades after he graced the racetracks.

A Champion's Tale

Dancing Brave's journey to becoming a champion was a saga of talent, dedication, and unwavering belief in his abilities. His rise from a grey foal in Newmarket to a classic-winning colt was just the beginning. The chapters that followed would solidify his status as one of the greatest racehorses of his time.

The Consistency of Greatness

One of the defining qualities of a true champion is consistency, and Dancing Brave exemplified this trait throughout his career. His performances were not flashes of brilliance followed by mediocrity; they were a steady stream of excellence. Race after race, he showcased his ability to produce remarkable performances, often with breathtaking turns of foot.

A Global Ambassador

Dancing Brave's impact was not confined to the United Kingdom; it extended across borders. His victories in prestigious international races, such as the Prix de l'Arc de Triomphe, showcased his ability to excel on the global stage. He became a global ambassador for British racing, a horse whose reputation extended far beyond his home turf.

The 1986 Eclipse Stakes

Dancing Brave's reputation as a champion was solidified in the 1986 Eclipse Stakes, a race that pitted him against a formidable field that included such stalwarts as Time Charter and Triptych. The race was a showcase of talent, and Dancing Brave's victory was a demonstration of his sheer brilliance.

The colt's turn of foot in the Eclipse Stakes left spectators in awe. His acceleration in the closing stages of the race was a testament to his exceptional abilities. It was a performance that added another layer to his legacy and left no doubt about his status as a champion.

The King George VI and Queen Elizabeth Stakes

The King George VI and Queen Elizabeth Stakes is one of the most prestigious races in British racing. Dancing Brave's victory in the 1986 edition was a remarkable achievement. The manner in which he overcame a strong field, including Solford and Shardari, highlighted his dominance.

Dancing Brave's performance in the King George VI and Queen Elizabeth Stakes was a defining moment in his career. It showcased his versatility and his ability to excel over a variety of distances. It was a race that further cemented his status as a champion who could conquer any challenge.

His Impact on the Sport

Dancing Brave's impact on the sport extended beyond the racetrack. His performances inspired a generation of horse racing enthusiasts and left an indelible mark on the history of the sport. The reverence with which he is spoken of today is a testament to the lasting impact he had on the world of horse racing.

His legacy as a champion lives on not just in records and statistics but in the stories and memories of those who had the privilege of witnessing his performances. His name is mentioned in the same breath as the greatest horses in the sport's history, and his enduring status as a champion is a reflection of his remarkable talent and the spirit of excellence that defined his career.

A Champion in Retrospect

As we explore Dancing Brave's enduring status as a champion, we delve into a chapter of racing history that remains relevant and inspiring. His story is a reminder that champions are not defined solely by their victories but by the impact they have on the sport and the legacy they leave behind. Dancing Brave's legacy endures, a beacon of excellence that continues to shine bright in the world of horse racing.

The Impact of Dancing Brave on the International Stage

While Dancing Brave's story is firmly rooted in British racing, his impact transcended national boundaries and left an indelible mark on the international stage. His performances abroad, his influence on global breeding, and his legacy as a true international champion are all testaments to his enduring significance.

A British Champion with Global Aspirations

Dancing Brave's journey from the Newmarket stables to the world stage was a testament to the universal appeal of thoroughbred racing. His initial success in the United Kingdom set the stage for a more ambitious plan: to compete on the international stage and showcase his exceptional abilities to a global audience.

The 1986 Prix de l'Arc de Triomphe Victory

Dancing Brave's victory in the 1986 Prix de l'Arc de Triomphe, held at Longchamp in France, remains one of the most iconic moments in the history of the race. The manner in which he dominated a field of international contenders was not just a win but a statement. It showcased that British racing was a force to be reckoned with on the global stage.

The Arc victory not only solidified his status as a champion but also introduced him to a worldwide audience.

The world took note of this exceptional grey colt and his remarkable turn of foot. The significance of his win went beyond a single race; it was a symbol of British racing's ability to produce horses of the highest caliber.

A Champion on the Continent

Dancing Brave's success in France was not a one-off. He continued to perform at the highest level on the continent. His performances in races such as the King George VI and Queen Elizabeth Stakes showcased his versatility and his ability to excel over a variety of distances.

His presence in international races added to the global appeal of British racing. His story was not just about a British champion but about a horse who could conquer challenges in different countries and conditions. His performances were a source of pride for British racing enthusiasts and an inspiration for breeders and horsemen around the world.

The Influence on Global Breeding

Dancing Brave's success had a profound impact on global breeding. His pedigree, which combined the bloodlines of Northern Dancer and Lyphard, became highly sought after. The influence of his lineage extended to breeding programs in various countries, leading to the production of horses with similar racing qualities.

His impact on international breeding was not limited to his immediate descendants but extended to subsequent generations. Horses with Dancing Brave in their pedigrees continued to achieve success on the global stage, further solidifying his legacy as a sire of champions.

A Legacy that Endures

Dancing Brave's legacy on the international stage endures to this day. His name is mentioned with reverence in discussions about the greatest racehorses of all time. His influence on global breeding continues to shape the pedigrees of top-class horses, and his performances remain a source of inspiration for those in the world of thoroughbred racing.

His impact was not just measured in wins and records; it was a testament to the global appeal of horse racing. It demonstrated that excellence in the sport knows no boundaries and that a champion can capture the hearts of enthusiasts around the world.

A Tribute to an International Icon

As we explore the impact of Dancing Brave on the international stage, we uncover a narrative that goes beyond the confines of a racetrack. It is a story of a horse who, through his performances and influence, became an international icon, a symbol of the universal appeal of horse racing, and a reminder that champions are revered not only in their home country but around the globe. Dancing Brave's legacy is a testament to the enduring power of the sport to unite people from diverse backgrounds in their admiration for a true equine hero.

Chapter 3: Zenyatta (United States, 2004-2020), Bay (appeared greyish in some light)
Zenyatta's Journey from Early Races to Becoming an Icon

Zenyatta, the iconic American mare who captured the hearts of racing enthusiasts, embarked on a remarkable journey from her early days in the world of horse racing to achieving the status of an icon. This chapter delves into the pivotal moments and races that defined her ascent to greatness.

A Humble Beginning

Zenyatta's journey began in 2004 when she was foaled at Winter Quarter Farm in Kentucky. As a daughter of Street Cry and Vertigineux, she had an impressive pedigree. However, her early days did not foreshadow the extraordinary career that awaited her.

Her early races were modest and took place on the California racing circuit. It was here that she displayed glimpses of her potential. Her early handlers recognized her talent, and she began to show her distinctive style of running from behind, often coming from far off the pace to secure victories.

The Unbeaten Streak

One of the defining aspects of Zenyatta's journey was her unbeaten streak, which began in 2007 and continued until her retirement in 2010. This remarkable run of 19 consecutive victories was a testament to her exceptional talent and consistent performances.

The streak included victories in prestigious races such as the Breeders' Cup Ladies' Classic, the Apple Blossom Handicap, and the Vanity Handicap. Each win added to her reputation and solidified her status as one of the most exceptional mares in the history of American horse racing.

The 2009 Breeders' Cup Classic

One of the most defining moments in Zenyatta's journey was her historic victory in the 2009 Breeders' Cup Classic. This race, known as the "Race of the Century," pitted her against a field of top-class male contenders. Zenyatta's performance in the Classic was not just a race; it was a moment that would be etched in the annals of horse racing history.

As she made her characteristic late charge, the crowd at Santa Anita Park roared with excitement. In a thrilling finish, Zenyatta overtook her rivals to remain unbeaten. Her victory was a celebration of talent, spirit, and the ability to transcend gender boundaries in racing.

The Legacy of a Racing Queen

Zenyatta's journey from early races to becoming an icon was not just about wins; it was about the hearts she touched. Her charisma extended beyond the racetrack, as she became a fan favorite. Her distinctive dance before races and her ability to connect with the audience made her a beloved figure.

Her impact was not limited to the United States. Zenyatta's performances were celebrated worldwide, and she earned fans from different corners of the globe. Her journey was a testament to the international appeal of horse racing and the ability of a great horse to bridge cultural divides.

A Milestone in Gender Equality

Zenyatta's journey was also a milestone in gender equality in horse racing. Her victories in top-class races, including the Breeders' Cup Classic, shattered the stereotype that top-level racing was reserved for male horses. She inspired a new generation of female jockeys, trainers, and owners, proving that greatness knows no gender.

The Legacy of an Icon

Zenyatta's journey from early races to becoming an icon is a story of talent, perseverance, and the ability to capture the collective imagination of racing enthusiasts. Her legacy endures not just in her record but in the inspiration she provided to those who dream of achieving greatness in the sport.

As we explore the various chapters of her remarkable journey, we come to understand that Zenyatta was more than a racehorse; she was a symbol of hope, a beacon of excellence, and a reminder that in the world of horse racing, the heart often races alongside the hooves. Her journey serves as an enduring tribute to the power of the equine spirit and its ability to touch lives around the world.

Her Unbeaten Streak and Breeders' Cup Classic Victory

Zenyatta's remarkable journey was marked by an unbeaten streak that captured the hearts of racing enthusiasts and culminated in a historic victory in the Breeders' Cup Classic. This chapter delves into the details of her unparalleled streak and the unforgettable moment when she etched her name in the annals of horse racing history.

The Beginnings of the Streak

Zenyatta's unbeaten streak began in her debut race at Hollywood Park in November 2007. From that moment, she embarked on a journey of consecutive victories that would leave an indelible mark on the sport. What made this streak truly remarkable was not just the number of wins but the quality of her competition and her ability to overcome challenging situations.

The Queen of Comebacks

One of Zenyatta's defining characteristics was her signature style of running from behind. She had a remarkable ability to make up ground in the latter stages of races, often thrilling spectators with her late charges. Her unique style set her apart and added an element of unpredictability to her races.

Race after race, Zenyatta would find herself trailing the field, seemingly out of contention. It was in these moments that her true greatness shone. Her late surges became the stuff of legends, and fans eagerly anticipated the heart-pounding finishes that became her trademark.

The Breeders' Cup Ladies' Classic

Zenyatta's journey to the Breeders' Cup Classic victory began with her stunning performance in the Breeders' Cup Ladies' Classic in 2008. This race showcased her ability to compete at the highest level against top-class fillies and mares.

Her victory in the Ladies' Classic marked the beginning of her association with the Breeders' Cup, an event that would become synonymous with her career. It was here that she captured the hearts of a wider audience and set the stage for the most iconic moment of her career.

The 2009 Breeders' Cup Classic

The 2009 Breeders' Cup Classic, held at Santa Anita Park, was a race that transcended the sport. It was more than just a race; it was a showdown of epic proportions. Zenyatta, the unbeaten mare, faced a field of top-class male contenders.

As the race unfolded, Zenyatta's late charge became a moment of racing history. With jockey Mike Smith aboard, she surged past her rivals in the closing stages of the race, thrilling the crowd and leaving spectators in awe. Her victory was not just a win; it was a symbol of her exceptional talent and the ability of a great racehorse to captivate the world.

A Celebration of Talent

Zenyatta's Breeders' Cup Classic victory was a celebration of her talent, her spirit, and her ability to transcend gender boundaries in racing. It was a moment that showcased the universal appeal of the sport and the power of a great racehorse to inspire people from different walks of life.

The victory in the Classic was more than just a race; it was a testament to Zenyatta's unique style and her ability to perform under pressure. It was a victory for all those who believed in her and for all those who saw in her the embodiment of excellence.

The Legacy of a Streak and a Classic Victory

Zenyatta's unbeaten streak and her Breeders' Cup Classic victory were not just moments in time; they were a legacy that endures in the hearts of racing enthusiasts. Her journey serves as a reminder that in the world of horse racing, greatness knows no boundaries, and champions are celebrated not only for their victories but for the inspiration they provide.

As we explore the remarkable tale of Zenyatta's unbeaten streak and Breeders' Cup Classic victory, we come to understand that her story is more than just a chapter in racing history; it is a testament to the enduring power of the equine spirit and its ability to create moments that transcend the sport itself. Zenyatta's legacy lives on, an eternal tribute to the magic of the racetrack.

The Global Recognition of a Beloved American Mare

Zenyatta, the remarkable American mare, transcended borders to become a beloved figure in the world of horse racing. This chapter explores the global recognition she received and the impact she had on racing enthusiasts around the world.

A Star is Born

Zenyatta's journey to global recognition began with her impressive performances on American racetracks. Her unbeaten streak and her signature style of coming from behind to win races captured the imagination of racing enthusiasts not only in the United States but around the world.

Her charisma and distinctive pre-race dance endeared her to fans. She was not just a racehorse; she was a star. The global recognition of her talent and personality started to take shape during her early racing days.

The International Appeal of the Breeders' Cup

The Breeders' Cup, an annual series of prestigious horse races, became a platform for Zenyatta to showcase her talent on the international stage. Her participation in the event drew the attention of racing enthusiasts from different countries. The Breeders' Cup was no longer just an American racing event; it had become a global spectacle.

Zenyatta's victories in the Breeders' Cup Ladies' Classic and the Breeders' Cup Classic catapulted her to international stardom. These wins showcased her ability to compete at the highest level and solidified her status as a global icon in the world of thoroughbred racing.

Fans from Around the World

Zenyatta's fan base extended far beyond the borders of the United States. Racing enthusiasts from various countries, including the United Kingdom, Australia, Japan, and many others, followed her career with fervor. Her captivating late charges and her unbeaten streak resonated with people from diverse backgrounds and cultures.

International racing publications and websites covered Zenyatta's races extensively. Her performances were dissected and analyzed by experts and fans alike, creating a global conversation about her greatness. The international racing community had found a common point of admiration in the American mare.

The Zenyatta Effect

Zenyatta's impact on the international racing scene was so profound that it became known as the "Zenyatta Effect." This referred to the phenomenon where she could attract spectators to the racetrack like no other. Her races were not just sporting events; they were spectacles, events that drew crowds and television viewers from around the world.

Her charismatic presence had the power to unite people in their appreciation for a great racehorse. Her races were watched in homes and bars, in different time zones, by fans who shared a common love for the sport. Zenyatta had become a global ambassador for horse racing.

A Symbol of Hope and Inspiration

Zenyatta's global recognition was not just about her victories; it was about the hope and inspiration she provided to people. She demonstrated that greatness could be achieved, even in the face of adversity. Her late charges in races became metaphors for overcoming challenges and obstacles in life.

Her impact extended to the younger generation of racing enthusiasts. Children and teenagers looked up to Zenyatta as a symbol of excellence. She encouraged them to dream big and believe in their abilities, whether in horse racing or in any other pursuit.

The Legacy of a Global Icon

Zenyatta's global recognition was not limited to her racing career. It extended to her retirement and her life as a broodmare. The foals she produced carried the legacy of their famous mother to various parts of the world, continuing the story of a beloved American mare.

As we explore the global recognition of Zenyatta, we come to understand that her impact on the world of horse racing was not confined to a single country. She was a symbol of the universal appeal of the sport and a reminder that excellence in the equine world knows no borders. Zenyatta's legacy lives on as a testament to the power of a great racehorse to inspire and unite people from different corners of the globe.

The Legacy of Zenyatta in the Hearts of Fans

Zenyatta's impact in the world of horse racing extended far beyond her time on the track. This chapter delves into the enduring legacy she left in the hearts of her fans, exploring the deep connection between the American mare and those who admired and adored her.

A Fan's Affection

Zenyatta was not just a racehorse; she was a phenomenon. Her unique style of racing, her charisma, and her undeniable talent earned her a special place in the hearts of racing enthusiasts. This section delves into the deep affection and admiration fans felt for the American mare.

The Zenyatta Nation

Zenyatta's fans, often referred to as the "Zenyatta Nation," were a passionate and devoted community. They transcended geographical boundaries and united in their shared love for the mare. Online forums, social media groups, and fan clubs brought together people from all walks of life who found common ground in their adoration of Zenyatta.

The "Zenyatta Nation" was not just a group of fans; it was a family. Members supported one another, celebrated victories together, and consoled each other in defeats.

Zenyatta had become more than a racehorse; she was a unifying force that connected people from around the world.

The Zenyatta Dance

One of the enduring symbols of Zenyatta's connection with her fans was her pre-race "dance." Before each race, Zenyatta would exhibit a distinctive and rhythmic dance that became her trademark. Fans eagerly awaited this ritual, and it became a shared moment of anticipation and excitement.

The "Zenyatta Dance" was more than just a pre-race routine; it was a connection between the mare and her fans. It was a moment when she acknowledged the crowd and the crowd acknowledged her. It was a symbol of the emotional bond that existed between Zenyatta and those who cheered for her.

Collective Joy and Tears

Zenyatta's races were not just sporting events; they were emotional roller coasters for her fans. The joy of her victories and the heartache of her narrow defeats were collectively experienced. Her races were moments of elation and, at times, tears, as fans rode the emotional journey alongside her.

Each race was a shared experience. Whether at the racetrack, in front of a television, or through live-streamed broadcasts, fans came together to witness Zenyatta's performances. Her races were a reminder that the beauty of the sport lay not just in the victories but in the shared emotions they evoked.

The Zenyatta Effect

The "Zenyatta Effect" extended to the broader racing community. She inspired artists, writers, and photographers to capture her essence. Her image appeared on posters, in books, and in works of art. The impact she had on the creative world was a testament to the depth of her influence.

Legacy Beyond Racing

Zenyatta's legacy was not confined to the racetrack. It extended to her life as a broodmare. The foals she produced carried the hopes and expectations of her fans. Each new generation of Zenyatta's descendants continued the story, creating a legacy that transcended generations.

Zenyatta's foals, including Cozmic One and Ziconic, became the new torchbearers of her legacy. Fans eagerly followed their racing careers, hoping to see glimpses of their famous mother in their performances.

An Eternal Connection

The legacy of Zenyatta in the hearts of her fans endures to this day. Her memory is kept alive through fan clubs, social media groups, and annual events that celebrate her greatness. Her impact on the racing community remains a source of inspiration for current and future generations.

Zenyatta's story is a testament to the unique and profound connection that can exist between a racehorse and those who admire her. It is a reminder that in the world of horse racing, it is not just about the races and the victories; it is also about the shared experiences and the lasting bonds that are formed between a remarkable horse and her adoring fans. Zenyatta will forever remain a cherished and beloved figure in the hearts of those who had the privilege of witnessing her greatness.

Chapter 4: Nashwan (United Kingdom, 1986-2002), Grey

Nashwan's Early Career and the Path to Becoming a Champion

Nashwan, the striking grey colt, embarked on a journey that would ultimately lead him to be recognized as one of the greatest racehorses of his time. This chapter delves into his early days and the crucial steps that paved the way for his ascent to champion status.

A Star in the Making

Nashwan was born in 1986 at Shadwell Stud, United Kingdom. His breeding was impeccable, with an illustrious lineage that included the likes of Blushing Groom and Height of Fashion. From an early age, he displayed a remarkable presence and an air of greatness.

As a foal, Nashwan's striking grey coat immediately caught the eye. His appearance was regal, and it hinted at the exceptional horse he would become. His early days were spent at the stud, where he began his journey to racing stardom.

Early Training and Development

Nashwan's early training and development played a crucial role in shaping his racing career. Under the guidance of expert trainers and handlers, he honed his racing skills.

His natural athleticism and eagerness to learn set him apart from his peers.

His workouts on the gallops revealed his potential. He displayed speed, agility, and a willingness to push himself in training. It became evident that Nashwan was not an ordinary horse; he was destined for greatness.

Debut on the Racetrack

Nashwan's debut on the racetrack was highly anticipated. As a well-bred colt with a promising training record, he had captured the attention of racing enthusiasts and punters. His first race marked the beginning of a journey that would captivate the racing world.

The race, held at Newmarket, was a showcase of his talent. Nashwan's victory in his debut race sent a clear message: a new star had arrived on the British racing scene. His charisma and style of running from the front thrilled spectators, and his potential was evident to all who watched.

The 2,000 Guineas Triumph

One of the pivotal moments in Nashwan's early career was his victory in the 2,000 Guineas, a prestigious classic race. The 2,000 Guineas was a test of speed and stamina, and it attracted top-class colts from around the country.

Nashwan's performance in the 2,000 Guineas was nothing short of spectacular. He displayed a brilliant turn of foot and surged ahead of his rivals in the closing stages of the race. The victory in this classic race was a defining moment that solidified his status as a classic contender and marked him as a potential champion.

Epsom Derby Glory

Nashwan's journey to champion status reached new heights with his victory in the Epsom Derby. The Derby is one of the most prestigious races in British racing and a true test of a three-year-old's class and ability to stay the distance.

Nashwan's performance in the Epsom Derby was a display of sheer dominance. He conquered the challenging course with ease, leaving his rivals trailing behind. The victory in the Derby was a testament to his versatility and his ability to excel over different distances.

International Recognition

Nashwan's success was not confined to British racing. He garnered international recognition and became a symbol of excellence on the global stage. His victories in the 2,000 Guineas and the Epsom Derby added to his reputation, making him a horse to watch for in international competitions.

His early career had laid the foundation for his international triumphs. The exceptional training, the regal pedigree, and the impressive debut race all contributed to his journey to becoming a champion. Nashwan's ascent to stardom was a testament to his innate talent and the careful guidance of his trainers and handlers.

A Glimpse into Greatness

As we explore Nashwan's early career and the path that led him to becoming a champion, we gain a glimpse into the making of a true racing legend. His story is a reminder that greatness is not achieved overnight but through a combination of talent, training, and the unwavering belief in a horse's potential. Nashwan's journey from a promising foal to a classic champion is a story of excellence that continues to inspire those in the world of horse racing.

His 1989 Epsom Derby Victory and 2000 Guineas Triumph

Nashwan's remarkable journey to greatness continued with his iconic victories in the 1989 Epsom Derby and the 2,000 Guineas. This chapter delves into the details of these prestigious wins, which solidified his status as a true champion in the world of horse racing.

The 1989 Epsom Derby: A Classic Triumph

The Epsom Derby, often referred to as "The Derby," is one of the most prestigious and historic horse races in the world. Nashwan's participation in this classic event was a defining moment in his career.

The Run-up to the Derby

Leading up to the Epsom Derby, Nashwan's reputation as a formidable contender had grown. His victory in the 2,000 Guineas had showcased his speed and stamina, making him a popular choice among punters and racing enthusiasts.

The Race Day Atmosphere

The atmosphere at Epsom Downs on Derby day was electric. Thousands of spectators had gathered to witness the race, and the tension was palpable. Nashwan's appearance in the parade ring was met with anticipation and excitement.

The Performance

Nashwan's performance in the Epsom Derby was nothing short of spectacular. The challenging course, with its undulating terrain and tight turns, often separates the great from the good. Nashwan proved himself more than capable, displaying a turn of foot that left his rivals struggling to catch up.

The final furlongs of the race saw Nashwan surge ahead with remarkable speed and grace. Jockey Willie Carson guided him to victory, and the roar of the crowd echoed through the Downs. Nashwan's triumph in the Epsom Derby was a moment of racing history, and he joined the elite ranks of horses that had conquered this iconic race.

The 2000 Guineas Triumph: A Classic Double

Following his Epsom Derby victory, Nashwan's next goal was the 2,000 Guineas, a classic race that tests a horse's speed and class over a mile. His participation in this race was highly anticipated.

Preparation and Expectation

The build-up to the 2,000 Guineas was marked by high expectations. Nashwan's Epsom Derby win had firmly established him as a classic contender, and racing enthusiasts were eager to see if he could achieve the rare feat of winning both classics.

The Race Day Drama

The 2,000 Guineas unfolded with all the drama and excitement expected of a classic race. A field of top-class colts and a fervent crowd awaited the start. Nashwan's grey coat shone under the spring sun, and he exuded an air of confidence.

Victory in Style

Nashwan's performance in the 2,000 Guineas was a display of his versatility. He demonstrated his ability to excel over varying distances. His acceleration in the closing stages of the race showcased his class and confirmed his status as a classic double winner.

The victory in the 2,000 Guineas was a testament to Nashwan's exceptional talent and his trainer's expertise in preparing him for classic races. It was a moment of pure class and elegance, leaving spectators in awe of his abilities.

A Dual Classic Champion

Nashwan's victories in both the Epsom Derby and the 2,000 Guineas were a testament to his versatility and brilliance. He had achieved a rare feat, becoming a dual classic champion and joining the elite ranks of British racing legends.

His dual classic triumph solidified his status as one of the greatest racehorses of his time. Nashwan's performances in these prestigious races showcased his exceptional ability to conquer both the mile and the demanding distance of the Derby. His victories were celebrated not only in the United Kingdom but also around the world, marking him as a true champion on the international stage.

The Legacy of a Classic Champion

As we explore Nashwan's 1989 Epsom Derby victory and his 2,000 Guineas triumph, we come to understand the significance of these classic wins in his journey to greatness. They were moments of pure racing excellence, testaments to his extraordinary talent, and memories that continue to inspire those who are captivated by the world of horse racing. Nashwan's legacy as a classic champion endures, and his name is forever etched in the annals of the sport's history.

The International Recognition of Nashwan's Greatness

Nashwan's achievements on the British turf resonated far beyond the United Kingdom. His extraordinary talent and classic victories captured the attention of the international racing community. In this chapter, we explore the global acclaim that Nashwan received and how he became a symbol of excellence on the international stage.

A British Champion with Global Appeal

Nashwan's emergence as a British racing sensation was swift and captivating. His classic wins, particularly in the Epsom Derby and the 2,000 Guineas, showcased his versatility and brilliance. These victories were celebrated not only by British racing enthusiasts but also by an international audience.

Media Coverage and Global Interest

Nashwan's triumphs received extensive media coverage, and racing publications worldwide recognized his exceptional talent. His victories were discussed in racing circles across Europe, North America, and even in racing-mad nations like Australia and Japan. Racing fans and experts from different corners of the globe started to take notice.

Appeal in Continental Europe

Nashwan's success had a particular impact on continental Europe. His Epsom Derby victory drew parallels with the revered Prix de l'Arc de Triomphe, the continent's premier horse race. European racing fans saw Nashwan as a potential challenger in the Arc and eagerly awaited his possible participation.

The Hype Leading to the Prix de l'Arc de Triomphe

The Prix de l'Arc de Triomphe, held at Longchamp in Paris, was one of the most prestigious horse races in Europe. Nashwan's potential entry in the race created immense excitement and anticipation. European racing enthusiasts were eager to see if the British champion could conquer their premier event.

Nashwan's Style and Versatility

Nashwan's ability to excel at varying distances and his electrifying turn of foot made him a captivating contender. His participation in the Arc was highly anticipated, and the discussions about his racing style and chances intensified.

Nashwan's Participation in the Prix de l'Arc de Triomphe

Nashwan's entry into the 1989 Prix de l'Arc de Triomphe marked a historic moment in European racing. The race featured a strong field of international contenders, and Nashwan was one of the British hopes.

The Performance

Nashwan's performance in the Prix de l'Arc de Triomphe was exceptional. He showcased his class and versatility by finishing a close second, narrowly missing out on victory. His performance earned him immense respect from European racing fans, and he had become a favorite on both sides of the English Channel.

The Global Legacy of Nashwan

Nashwan's international recognition extended beyond his racing career. His legacy as a champion and a symbol of excellence in thoroughbred racing was felt worldwide. Racing enthusiasts from different countries revered him for his remarkable achievements and versatile racing style.

Influence on Breeding and Racing Styles

Nashwan's breeding career left a lasting impact. His bloodline became highly sought after, and his offspring carried the legacy of their famous sire. His genes were spread across the globe, and his influence on the breeding and racing styles of future generations was undeniable.

Legacy of Versatility

Nashwan's legacy was not confined to the United Kingdom or Europe. His versatility as a racehorse and his success in varying distances inspired horsemen and women worldwide. His story became a testament to the universal appeal of horse racing and the ability of a great racehorse to transcend borders.

The Enduring Recognition of Nashwan

As we explore the international recognition of Nashwan's greatness, we come to understand the significance of his impact on the global racing community. Nashwan's journey from a British classic champion to a celebrated figure in international racing showcased the universal allure of the sport and the ability of a great racehorse to capture the hearts of fans worldwide. His legacy endures as a reminder that excellence in the world of horse racing knows no boundaries, and true champions are celebrated on the world stage.

His Enduring Presence in the History of Horse Racing

Nashwan's legacy extends far beyond his racing career. In this chapter, we explore how his remarkable achievements, distinctive grey coat, and captivating racing style secured his enduring presence in the annals of horse racing history. Nashwan remains a revered figure whose impact on the sport transcends time and borders.

A Name Enshrined in History

Nashwan's name is etched in the annals of horse racing history. His classic victories, notably in the Epsom Derby and the 2,000 Guineas, elevated him to a place of prominence in the pantheon of racing greats. His achievements are celebrated and remembered by generations of racing enthusiasts.

The Epsom Derby: A Historic Triumph

Nashwan's victory in the Epsom Derby was a historic moment in British racing. The Derby, known for its rich tradition and legacy, had witnessed countless champions, but Nashwan's name now stood among them. His triumph in this prestigious race secured his place in the lineage of Derby winners, and his performance is frequently revisited in discussions of the event's most iconic moments.

The Dual Classic Champion

Nashwan's rare accomplishment of winning both the Epsom Derby and the 2,000 Guineas in the same year is a testament to his exceptional talent and versatility. The significance of this dual classic victory is remembered not only as a sporting achievement but as a symbol of racing greatness.

His victories in these classics are studied and celebrated by racing historians, and they serve as a reference point for assessing the performances of subsequent generations of racehorses. Nashwan's dual classic win remains a remarkable feat in the history of British racing.

A Champion in Grey

Nashwan's distinctive grey coat added to his allure. The rarity of grey horses in racing made him a visually striking figure on the track. His grey coat, often glistening under the sunlight, became an iconic symbol of his presence in the sport.

Fans and photographers sought to capture the beauty of the grey champion in action. His images adorn racing books, magazines, and websites, keeping his memory alive in the hearts of those who admire his unique appearance.

An International Figure

Nashwan's international recognition expanded his presence on the global stage. His participation in the Prix de l'Arc de Triomphe and his performance in that prestigious race solidified his status as an international racing figure. He became a name recognized not only in the United Kingdom but in racing circles around the world.

Influence on Breeding

Nashwan's influence as a stallion and sire was significant. His offspring continued to carry his legacy, both in appearance and talent. His impact on the breeding world contributed to his enduring presence, as generations of racehorses inherited his bloodlines and characteristics.

Legacy of Versatility and Excellence

Nashwan's legacy is one of versatility and excellence. He showcased the ability of a racehorse to excel in varying distances and on different types of racetracks. His story serves as an inspiration for trainers, jockeys, and breeders who strive for excellence and versatility in the world of horse racing.

Continued Reverence

Nashwan's enduring presence is reflected in the continued reverence he receives from the racing community. His memory is celebrated through annual events, articles, and discussions about the greatest racehorses in history. He remains a cherished figure, and his legacy is passed down to new generations of racing enthusiasts.

Nashwan's place in the history of horse racing is secured not only by his remarkable performances but by the indelible mark he left on the sport. His enduring presence serves as a reminder of the timeless appeal of horse racing and the capacity of a true champion to leave a lasting legacy that transcends the boundaries of time and geography.

Chapter 5: Global Triumphs Unveiled
Exploring the Global Feats of These Iconic Racehorses

This chapter is a journey across the world of horse racing, as we delve into the global accomplishments of the iconic racehorses featured in this book. Their remarkable feats extended beyond their home countries, and their international triumphs became legendary in the world of thoroughbred racing.

Legends Without Borders

The iconic racehorses discussed in this book were not confined by national boundaries. They transcended borders to achieve greatness on the global stage. This section introduces the idea of horse racing as a truly international sport, with champions who capture the hearts of fans around the world.

Champion vs. Champion: International Showdowns

In the world of horse racing, international showdowns between champions are moments of pure excitement. These races attract attention from all corners of the globe as fans eagerly anticipate the meeting of two or more iconic racehorses.

We explore some of the most memorable international showdowns in which our featured horses participated. These races were not just about victory but about the thrill of seeing the best from different nations competing against each other.

Breaking Course Records Around the World

Another fascinating aspect of the global feats of these racehorses is their ability to break course records on different tracks. Each track has its unique challenges, and setting records on diverse courses requires exceptional talent and adaptability.

We delve into specific instances where our featured horses set new course records, demonstrating their versatility and capability to conquer unfamiliar terrain.

Global Racing Tours: Iconic Horses on World Stages

Some of our featured racehorses embarked on international racing tours, where they competed on multiple continents. These tours showcased their exceptional abilities and their capacity to adapt to various racing conditions.

We follow the journeys of these horses as they traveled the world, taking on top competitors from different regions and leaving a trail of admirers in their wake.

International Recognition and Awards

Winning international awards and accolades is a testament to a horse's global impact. We explore the prestigious awards our featured horses received, such as the

Longines World's Best Racehorse Award, which recognizes the world's top racehorses.

These accolades demonstrate that the iconic racehorses were not just local heroes; they were celebrated on a global scale, earning the respect and admiration of fans, horsemen, and racing authorities worldwide.

Their Lasting Impact on Global Horse Racing

The global feats of the iconic racehorses did not end with their retirements. Their lasting impact on the world of horse racing continues to influence the sport. We discuss the ways in which their achievements have shaped the industry, from breeding trends to the way international racing events are organized.

Their legacies extend far beyond their racing careers, serving as a source of inspiration for new generations of racehorses and a reminder of the enduring appeal of the sport of kings on a global scale.

The Impact of Their International Success and Recognition

In this section, we explore the profound influence that the international success and recognition of iconic racehorses have had on the world of horse racing. These horses transcended borders, and their impact reached far beyond their home countries.

Elevating the Prestige of International Races

The international success of iconic racehorses has elevated the prestige of races worldwide. We examine how these horses, by participating in and winning prestigious races on different continents, transformed these events into global spectacles.

Races like the Prix de l'Arc de Triomphe, the Dubai World Cup, and the Breeders' Cup gained international acclaim, attracting top-class horses from around the world. Iconic racehorses played a pivotal role in this transformation by setting new standards of excellence and making these races must-watch events on the global racing calendar.

Attracting a Global Fanbase

The global recognition of iconic racehorses drew fans from diverse backgrounds into the world of horse racing. We discuss how the allure of these horses transcended national boundaries, bringing together a community of fans with a shared passion for the sport.

Online fan groups, international fan clubs, and social media communities formed around these horses, fostering connections among fans from different countries. The impact of these horses on the growth of the global racing community cannot be underestimated.

Inspiring International Ownership

The international success of iconic racehorses inspired owners and breeders to participate in the global racing circuit. We explore how the achievements of these horses encouraged individuals and syndicates to invest in thoroughbreds with the potential to compete on the international stage.

This led to increased international ownership and the exchange of bloodlines across borders, further enriching the global racing landscape. Iconic horses not only inspired fans but also fueled the ambitions of those involved in the industry.

International Collaborations and Exchanges

The recognition of these iconic racehorses as global champions fostered collaborations and exchanges within the racing community. We delve into instances where trainers, jockeys, and breeding experts from different countries came together to maximize the potential of top-class horses.

International collaborations often led to innovative training methods, the sharing of racing expertise, and the blending of different racing traditions. These exchanges enriched the sport and contributed to the continued success of iconic racehorses.

Economic Impact on the Racing Industry

The international recognition of iconic racehorses also had a substantial economic impact on the racing industry. We discuss how the increased attention and investments resulting from their success led to the growth of the sport's economic ecosystem.

From breeding operations to race sponsorship deals and tourism, the global appeal of these horses enhanced the industry's financial viability. Their impact reverberated throughout the racing world, supporting jobs and businesses connected to the sport.

Global Promotion of Horse Racing

The international recognition of iconic racehorses played a pivotal role in promoting horse racing as a global sport. We examine how their stories were used to attract new audiences and drive interest in racing, not only as a sporting endeavor but also as a cultural and entertainment experience.

These horses became ambassadors for the sport, featured in international marketing campaigns and documentaries that showcased the beauty and excitement of horse racing. Their influence reached far beyond the racing community, contributing to a broader appreciation of the sport.

Transcending Generations

The legacy of iconic racehorses continues to transcend generations. We explore how these horses are celebrated as symbols of excellence and how their stories are passed down to new generations of racing enthusiasts.

Their impact on the sport remains relevant today, serving as a source of inspiration for owners, trainers, jockeys, and fans. Iconic racehorses are not simply figures from the past; they are living legends whose influence endures in the present and into the future.

The international success and recognition of these iconic racehorses have left an indelible mark on the world of horse racing, shaping its global landscape and ensuring that their legacies will continue to captivate the hearts and minds of racing enthusiasts worldwide.

The Unique Qualities That Set Them Apart on the Global Stage

In this section, we delve into the exceptional qualities that distinguished the iconic racehorses featured in this book on the global racing stage. These unique attributes and characteristics not only made them champions in their respective countries but also earned them recognition and admiration worldwide.

Unparalleled Consistency

One of the standout qualities that set these iconic racehorses apart was their unparalleled consistency. We explore how these horses could maintain their form over extended periods, resulting in impressive winning streaks that captured the imagination of fans around the world.

From Winx's astonishing 33-race win streak to Zenyatta's unbeaten record, we examine how consistency was a hallmark of their careers, making them beloved figures not just in their home countries but on the global racing scene.

Versatility Across Distances

The ability to excel at varying distances is a rare quality that distinguishes great racehorses. We discuss how our featured horses showcased their versatility by winning races at different distances, from sprints to classic distances.

Nashwan's victories in the 2,000 Guineas and the Epsom Derby, which represent different racing challenges, demonstrate his adaptability and class. Dancing Brave's ability to win over both shorter and longer distances showcased his remarkable versatility. We delve into how these horses' versatility made them global icons.

Majestic Racing Styles

Each of the featured horses had a distinctive racing style that captured the hearts of fans. We explore the majestic styles of these horses, from Winx's explosive turn of foot to Nashwan's front-running flair and Zenyatta's late, dramatic charges.

Their unique racing styles not only made them thrilling to watch but also established them as horses with charisma and a rare connection with their audiences. These qualities transcended borders, making them favorites worldwide.

Grace Under Pressure

The ability to perform under pressure is a quality that defines champions. We discuss how these iconic racehorses exhibited grace and composure in high-stakes races, often with the world watching.

Their remarkable performances in events like the Prix de l'Arc de Triomphe and the Breeders' Cup Classic, where the pressure was intense, demonstrated their character and mental fortitude. Their ability to handle pressure and perform at the highest level on the global stage became an enduring part of their legacies.

Strong Connections with Fans

The bond between these iconic racehorses and their fans was a unique quality that set them apart. We explore how their engaging personalities, connections with jockeys, and accessibility to fans through public events and social media endeared them to a global audience.

Fans from different countries felt a personal connection with these horses, and their presence at races, parades, and meet-and-greet sessions made them beloved figures worldwide.

Enduring Beauty and Grace

The physical attributes of these horses were also a source of fascination. We discuss how their striking appearances, such as Nashwan's regal grey coat, Winx's gleaming bay coat, and Zenyatta's elegance, contributed to their unique appeal.

Their beauty and grace were not only celebrated in the world of horse racing but also by artists, photographers, and the wider public. They became symbols of equine beauty and power, transcending their roles as racehorses to become cultural icons.

A Lasting Legacy

The unique qualities that set these horses apart on the global stage ensured that their legacies endure. We explore how these horses' exceptional attributes continue to inspire new generations of racehorses, leaving a lasting impact on the sport of horse racing.

Their stories are a reminder that greatness knows no borders and that truly exceptional racehorses have qualities that resonate with fans around the world. These horses are not just icons of their time but legends whose unique attributes continue to captivate the hearts and minds of racing enthusiasts globally.

Chapter 6: The World's Jockeys: Partners in Glory Recognizing the Jockeys Who Played Crucial Roles in These Horses' International Triumphs

In this section, we pay homage to the talented jockeys who formed integral partnerships with the iconic racehorses featured in this book. These jockeys were not mere passengers but skilled pilots who guided these exceptional equine athletes to international success and recognition.

The Jockey-Horse Connection

We explore the profound bond between jockeys and their mounts, emphasizing that this partnership is at the heart of horse racing. The symbiotic relationship between jockey and horse is crucial to achieving greatness on the global stage.

Profiles in Partnership: Jockeys on the World Stage

We present profiles of the jockeys who played pivotal roles in the international triumphs of our featured horses. These profiles offer insights into the backgrounds, careers, and racing styles of these remarkable jockeys.

Australia's Jockey Royalty: Hugh Bowman and Winx

Hugh Bowman's partnership with Winx is a case study in the remarkable connection between a jockey and a horse. We explore Bowman's journey, his collaboration with Winx, and the role he played in her unprecedented 33-race win streak.

International Success: Pat Eddery and Dancing Brave

Pat Eddery's international racing career and his partnership with Dancing Brave are discussed in depth. We examine how Eddery's experience in different racing jurisdictions contributed to Dancing Brave's global appeal and success.

American Legend: Mike E. Smith and Zenyatta

Mike E. Smith's extraordinary career and his partnership with Zenyatta, a beloved American mare, are profiled. We explore how Smith's tactical brilliance and understanding of his mount elevated Zenyatta to international stardom.

The British Maestro: Willie Carson and Nashwan

Willie Carson's role in Nashwan's victories is a central focus. We delve into Carson's legendary career, his relationship with Nashwan, and his contributions to the grey champion's international recognition.

Strategies and Tactics in International Races

We examine the strategies and tactics employed by these jockeys in international races. Each jockey had a unique approach that contributed to their horse's success on the global stage. From riding style to race awareness, we explore how these jockeys made a difference in their horse's victories.

Mental Toughness and Pressure Handling

International races often come with immense pressure. We discuss how these jockeys demonstrated remarkable mental toughness and the ability to perform under high-stress conditions. Their composure in crucial moments played a pivotal role in securing international triumphs.

Overcoming Challenges Abroad

Riding in foreign countries presents its own set of challenges, from adapting to different tracks to understanding local racing cultures. We explore how these jockeys overcame these challenges and navigated their horses to victory in international races.

The Global Impact of Jockey Success

The success of these jockeys on the international stage had a significant impact not only on their careers but on the broader racing community. We discuss how their victories in prestigious international races elevated their status and influenced future generations of jockeys.

Fans and Connections

The connection between fans and jockeys is explored, emphasizing how these jockeys became beloved figures in their own right. Their stories, their interactions with fans, and their contributions to the sport's global appeal are highlighted.

The Enduring Legacy of Jockey-Horse Partnerships

The legacies of these jockey-horse partnerships continue to inspire new generations of racing enthusiasts. We reflect on the lasting impact of these partnerships and their role in making the sport of horse racing a global spectacle. The connections between jockeys and horses are celebrated as an essential part of racing's enduring allure.

The Connections and International Collaborations That Contributed to Their Success

In this section, we delve into the connections and collaborations that played a crucial role in the international success of iconic racehorses. These partnerships extended beyond the jockey-horse relationship and involved trainers, owners, and even international experts who contributed to the horses' triumphs on the global stage.

The Global Racing Network

We explore the expansive network of individuals and organizations that are essential to the global racing industry. From breeders to trainers, owners to race organizers, these connections form the backbone of international racing.

Trainers and Their Expertise

The role of trainers in preparing racehorses for international campaigns is pivotal. We discuss the trainers who shaped the careers of our featured horses and examine how their expertise in conditioning and strategy played a crucial role in achieving international success.

Trainer Profiles: The Mentors Behind the Champions

We present profiles of the trainers who guided these iconic racehorses to international acclaim. These profiles offer insights into the training methods, strategies, and philosophies that were instrumental in preparing the horses for their global campaigns.

Owners and Their Vision

The vision and commitment of owners are explored, as their decisions often shape the racing careers of horses. We discuss the owners who supported and believed in the global potential of these horses, making significant investments to ensure their success on international stages.

Owner Profiles: The Stewards of Racing Dreams

We provide profiles of the owners who played key roles in the international journeys of these horses. These profiles shed light on the vision, dedication, and love for the sport that drove these individuals to invest in the global racing ambitions of their equine partners.

International Collaboration and Exchange of Expertise

We examine instances of international collaboration in the world of horse racing, where trainers, owners, and experts from different countries came together to optimize the horses' potential.

Examples of International Collaborations: How Connections Transcended Borders

We delve into specific examples of collaborations that contributed to the horses' international success. These might include partnerships between owners from different countries, trainers with international experience, or the exchange of knowledge between racing jurisdictions.

Training Camps and Overseas Campaigns

To prepare horses for international races, many underwent training camps and overseas campaigns. We explore the significance of these endeavors, from acclimatizing horses to different environments to exposing them to new racing conditions.

Specialist Support Teams

The support teams that surrounded these horses are highlighted, including veterinarians, farriers, physiotherapists, and nutritionists. We discuss the role of these specialists in maintaining the horses' health, fitness, and performance during international campaigns.

Strategies for International Racing Success

The strategies employed by connections to ensure international racing success are examined. This includes race selection, travel plans, acclimatization, and the timing of international campaigns.

The Global Racing Community

The connections and collaborations that contributed to the international success of iconic racehorses are a testament to the global racing community's interconnectedness. We discuss how the exchange of expertise, the forging of international partnerships, and the shared passion for the sport have made horse racing a truly global endeavor.

The Enduring Legacy of Connections

The legacy of these connections lives on in the world of horse racing. Their contributions to the success of iconic racehorses continue to inspire the next generation of racing professionals, reinforcing the idea that success on the global stage is a collaborative effort that transcends borders and showcases the universal appeal of the sport.

The Challenges and Triumphs Faced by Horse and Rider Across Different Nations

In this section, we delve into the challenges and triumphs experienced by both the horse and the jockey as they navigated the international racing circuit. Racing in different nations brought unique hurdles and rewards, ultimately contributing to their global success.

Crossing Borders: The International Racing Experience

We set the stage by discussing the significance of international racing and the allure of competing in different nations. The global racing experience is celebrated as a testament to the diversity and universality of the sport.

Logistical Challenges

International racing involves complex logistics, from arranging travel for horses to coordinating quarantine and transportation. We explore the logistical challenges faced by horses and the support teams that accompanied them on their journeys.

Behind the Scenes: The Global Logistics of Horse Travel

We provide insights into the intricate logistics of transporting racehorses across borders. This includes considerations of quarantine, air travel, and the coordination required for a successful international campaign.

Acclimatization and Training Abroad

Adapting to different racing conditions and climates is a significant challenge for both horse and rider. We examine how horses and jockeys acclimatized to new environments, including different track surfaces and weather conditions.

Training Camps and Overseas Preparations: The Key to Adaptation

We discuss the role of training camps and overseas preparations in helping horses and riders adjust to new environments. These initiatives were crucial in ensuring that the horses were in peak condition for their international campaigns.

Navigating Different Tracks and Racing Styles

Racing on foreign tracks introduces horses and jockeys to unfamiliar challenges. We explore how they adjusted to different track configurations, racing styles, and competition standards.

Track Profiles: From Epsom Downs to Meydan's Turf

We provide profiles of the international tracks on which our featured horses competed. These profiles highlight the unique characteristics and challenges of each course, from the undulating terrain of Epsom Downs to the state-of-the-art facilities at Dubai's Meydan.

Cultural and Language Barriers

International racing often meant encountering diverse cultures and languages. We discuss how horses and riders dealt with cultural differences and the role of interpreters and international connections in facilitating communication.

The Cultural Exchange: From Royal Ascot to the Dubai World Cup

We explore how international racing brought horses and riders into contact with different racing traditions and cultures, from the pageantry of Royal Ascot to the opulence of the Dubai World Cup.

Supporting the Horses' Well-Being

The well-being of the horses was of paramount importance during international campaigns. We examine the efforts to maintain their health and happiness while competing abroad.

Veterinary and Wellness Care: Ensuring the Horses' Comfort

We discuss the role of veterinarians and wellness professionals in ensuring the health and happiness of the horses. This includes considerations such as jet lag, climate adaptation, and dietary adjustments.

Triumphs on the Global Stage

While international racing posed challenges, it also offered opportunities for remarkable triumphs. We celebrate the moments when horses and jockeys overcame adversity to achieve victory in foreign lands.

International Victories: A Showcase of Resilience

We recount specific international victories of our featured horses, highlighting the resilience and adaptability that led to their success. These moments are celebrated as the pinnacle of their global racing careers.

The Global Racing Spirit

The challenges and triumphs faced by horse and rider across different nations epitomize the global racing spirit. We discuss how these experiences enriched the world of horse racing and showcased the determination and adaptability of all those involved.

Enduring Lessons from International Campaigns

The lessons learned from international racing campaigns continue to inspire and inform the horse racing community. We reflect on the enduring legacy of these challenges and triumphs, emphasizing their role in shaping the sport's international appeal and universal allure.

Chapter 7: A Global Legacy Beyond Borders Celebrating the Records, Achievements, and Impact of These International Icons

In this section, we celebrate the remarkable records, achievements, and the lasting impact of the iconic racehorses featured in this book. Their feats on the global stage have left an indelible mark on the world of horse racing.

Records and Milestones

We begin by highlighting the exceptional records and milestones achieved by these iconic racehorses during their international careers. This section is dedicated to quantifying their greatness in terms of numbers and statistics.

Winx: The Record-Breaker from Down Under

We delve into Winx's record-breaking 33-race win streak, her impressive Cox Plate victories, and other milestones that solidified her place in racing history.

Dancing Brave: The Extraordinary Prix de l'Arc de Triomphe Victory

Dancing Brave's remarkable win in the 1986 Prix de l'Arc de Triomphe is celebrated as a defining moment in international racing history.

Zenyatta: The Unbeaten Champion of the Breeders' Cup Classic

We explore Zenyatta's unbeaten streak and her historic victory in the Breeders' Cup Classic, cementing her status as an American racing legend.

Nashwan: The Dual Classic Champion with a Global Presence

Nashwan's victories in the Epsom Derby and the 2,000 Guineas are showcased as feats of international significance.

Global Awards and Recognitions

The international recognition and awards received by these iconic racehorses are discussed, emphasizing their status as global racing icons.

Longines World's Best Racehorse Award: A Global Honor

We examine the significance of the Longines World's Best Racehorse Award, which recognizes the world's top racehorses. The horses' rankings and achievements in this prestigious award are highlighted.

A Lasting Impact on the Racing Industry

We explore the enduring impact of these horses on the racing industry, from their influence on breeding trends to the organization of international racing events.

Breeding Trends and the Continuation of Bloodlines

The legacy of these horses is evident in the bloodlines of future generations. We discuss how their genetics continue to shape the racing world, producing talented offspring with the potential for international success.

The Evolution of International Racing Events

The impact of these iconic racehorses on the development of international racing events is discussed. We highlight how their participation in and victories at prestigious races transformed these events into global spectacles.

Global Fan Engagement and Fan Clubs

The global fan engagement and the formation of fan clubs around these horses are celebrated. We discuss the enthusiastic following that these horses garnered from fans around the world.

Online Communities and Fan Gatherings

We explore the online communities and fan gatherings that brought together enthusiasts from different countries, fostering connections and camaraderie among fans of these iconic racehorses.

The Inspiration for New Generations

These iconic racehorses continue to inspire new generations of racehorses, trainers, jockeys, and fans. We reflect on the horses' roles as symbols of excellence and the source of motivation for the future of the sport.

Living Legends and Modern Inspirations

We discuss how these horses are celebrated as living legends and inspirations for those involved in horse racing. Their influence continues to shape the aspirations and dreams of the racing community.

The Global Racing Community's Connection to Unforgettable Champions

The global racing community is celebrated for its connection to these unforgettable champions. We emphasize the shared love and appreciation for these horses that transcends borders and unites racing enthusiasts worldwide.

The Legacy Endures

The records, achievements, and impact of these international icons serve as a reminder that greatness knows no borders. Their stories continue to captivate the hearts and minds of racing enthusiasts, ensuring that their legacy endures as a source of inspiration and admiration in the world of horse racing.

The Enduring Fascination and Love for 'Whispers of Mist and Triumph'

In this section, we explore the timeless fascination and love that 'Whispers of Mist and Triumph' has evoked in racing enthusiasts around the world. The book itself, dedicated to celebrating iconic racehorses with white and grey coats, has become a beloved part of the racing community's heritage.

A Tribute to the Icons

We begin by emphasizing that 'Whispers of Mist and Triumph' serves as a heartfelt tribute to the iconic racehorses who have graced the global racing stage. The book's purpose is not only to celebrate their achievements but to preserve their legacies for future generations.

The Global Appeal of the Book

We discuss how 'Whispers of Mist and Triumph' has transcended borders and resonated with readers from various countries and racing cultures. Its global appeal is attributed to the universal love for horses and the recognition of the featured horses' extraordinary feats.

The Book as a Source of Knowledge

We highlight how 'Whispers of Mist and Triumph' has served as an educational resource, providing racing enthusiasts with valuable insights into the careers of iconic horses. The book has deepened the knowledge of both seasoned fans and newcomers to the sport.

Collectors' Editions and Memorabilia

The special collectors' editions and associated memorabilia related to 'Whispers of Mist and Triumph' are explored. These items, which include limited edition prints, signed copies, and racehorse-themed merchandise, have become cherished collectibles among racing aficionados.

The Role of Fan Clubs

The formation of fan clubs dedicated to the featured horses and the book itself is discussed. These clubs have organized events, gatherings, and online forums, fostering a sense of community among fans who share a passion for the book's subjects.

Influence on Art and Culture

We explore how 'Whispers of Mist and Triumph' has influenced the world of art and culture. The iconic racehorses' stories have inspired artists, writers, and filmmakers, resulting in a rich tapestry of creative works that celebrate their legacies.

Inspiration for Future Generations

The book's role as an inspiration for future generations of racing enthusiasts, including young jockeys, trainers, and horse breeders, is celebrated. The stories of the iconic horses serve as a source of motivation for those looking to make their mark in the racing world.

Online Communities and Social Media

The role of online communities and social media in connecting fans of 'Whispers of Mist and Triumph' is highlighted. These platforms have facilitated discussions, fan-generated content, and the sharing of personal stories and experiences related to the book and its subjects.

Fan Letters and Personal Stories

We include excerpts from fan letters and personal stories shared by readers of 'Whispers of Mist and Triumph.' These heartwarming accounts reflect the emotional connection that fans have developed with the featured horses and the book.

The Legacy of 'Whispers of Mist and Triumph'

The enduring fascination and love for 'Whispers of Mist and Triumph' is celebrated as an integral part of the global racing community's heritage. The book's role in preserving the legacies of iconic racehorses and uniting racing enthusiasts from around the world underscores the timeless power of these remarkable horses to inspire, educate, and captivate the hearts of generations past, present, and future.

The Global Racing Community's Connection to These Unforgettable Champions

In this section, we celebrate the profound connection that the global racing community has with the iconic racehorses featured in 'Whispers of Mist and Triumph.' These horses have transcended borders and touched the hearts of enthusiasts around the world.

A Worldwide Fanbase

We emphasize the global reach of the fanbase that has formed around these iconic racehorses. Racing enthusiasts from diverse countries, cultures, and backgrounds have come together to celebrate their favorite champions.

United by a Shared Passion

The shared passion for horse racing serves as a unifying force that transcends national and cultural boundaries. We explore how the love for these horses has connected fans from all corners of the globe, creating a global racing family.

International Recognition and Appreciation

The international recognition and appreciation of these horses are discussed. We highlight how they are celebrated not just in their home countries but also in racing communities worldwide, receiving accolades and admiration from different parts of the globe.

Fan Gatherings and Global Events

We delve into the fan gatherings and global events that have celebrated the featured horses. These events, whether held at prestigious races or dedicated to specific champions, have provided fans with opportunities to connect and share their passion for racing.

Social Media and Online Communities

The role of social media and online communities in connecting fans across borders is explored. These platforms have allowed fans to come together, share experiences, and support their favorite horses, fostering a sense of camaraderie among racing enthusiasts.

International Fan Clubs

The formation of international fan clubs dedicated to specific horses is highlighted. These clubs have organized events, meetups, and collaborative projects that promote the horses' legacies and create a sense of belonging for fans worldwide.

Fan Letters and Testimonials

We include fan letters and testimonials from readers of 'Whispers of Mist and Triumph.' These heartfelt messages reflect the deep emotional connection that fans have developed with the iconic racehorses and their stories.

Global Fan Art and Creativity

The global outpouring of fan art, creative projects, and tributes dedicated to these horses is celebrated. We showcase how fans have expressed their admiration through artistic endeavors, further strengthening the bond between the racing community and the featured horses.

The Influence on New Generations

The impact of these iconic horses on inspiring new generations of racing enthusiasts is discussed. We explore how their stories serve as a source of motivation for young jockeys, trainers, breeders, and fans looking to be a part of the racing world.

The Global Legacy

The global racing community's connection to these unforgettable champions is a testament to the enduring appeal and universal admiration of these horses. Their legacies have become a shared heritage, uniting racing enthusiasts worldwide and ensuring that the stories of these remarkable champions continue to inspire, educate, and captivate the hearts of generations to come.

Conclusion

The Global Influence of White and Grey Icons

In this concluding section, we reflect on the profound global influence of the iconic white and grey racehorses featured in 'Whispers of Mist and Triumph.' Their legacies transcend borders, leaving an indelible mark on the world of horse racing and uniting enthusiasts from all corners of the globe.

A Universal Language: The Love of Horses

We begin by highlighting the universal appeal of horses and the profound connection they forge with people worldwide. The love of these majestic animals is a language understood by all, transcending cultural, linguistic, and geographical boundaries.

The Unique Allure of White and Grey Horses

We discuss the distinctive allure of white and grey coat colors in the racing world. These horses, with their striking and often rare appearances, have captured the imaginations of racing fans and stand out as symbols of uniqueness and distinction.

The Global Legacy of Iconic Racehorses

The enduring legacy of the iconic racehorses featured in 'Whispers of Mist and Triumph' is celebrated. Their stories have become an integral part of racing history, inspiring generations and leaving an everlasting impact on the sport.

Influence on Breeding and Bloodlines

We delve into how the bloodlines of these iconic horses have influenced the breeding industry. Their exceptional genetics continue to shape the future of racing, producing horses with the potential to achieve international acclaim.

The Evolution of International Racing Events

The impact of these horses on the international racing calendar is explored. Their participation in prestigious races has elevated these events to global spectacles, drawing attention and competitors from around the world.

Global Fan Engagement

The global fan engagement and the formation of fan communities dedicated to these horses are celebrated. The passion and enthusiasm of racing enthusiasts transcend borders, uniting fans in their shared admiration for the champions.

The Influence on Art and Culture

We reflect on how the stories of these iconic racehorses have influenced art, literature, and culture. Their narratives have inspired creative works that continue to honor their legacies and introduce their stories to new audiences.

The Legacy for Future Generations

The role of these horses as inspirations for future generations of racing enthusiasts is discussed. Their stories serve as a source of motivation for young jockeys, trainers, breeders, and fans looking to make their mark in the racing world.

A Global Community United by Racing

The global racing community's unity and shared love for these unforgettable champions underscore the profound influence of these horses. Racing enthusiasts from different nations and backgrounds are bound together by a common passion for the sport and the remarkable horses that have graced it.

The Timeless Power of Horse Racing

In closing, we emphasize the timeless power of horse racing to captivate hearts and minds. The iconic white and grey racehorses featured in 'Whispers of Mist and Triumph' serve as enduring symbols of excellence, beauty, and the universal allure of the sport.

The Legacy Lives On

As we conclude our journey through the remarkable stories of these equine heroes, we recognize that their legacies will continue to echo through time, inspiring new generations and perpetuating the global fascination with 'Whispers of Mist and Triumph.'

International Success and the Worldwide Racing Community

In this concluding section, we reflect on the theme of international success in horse racing and its profound impact on the worldwide racing community. The stories of iconic white and grey racehorses featured in 'Whispers of Mist and Triumph' exemplify the global nature of the sport and the universal admiration for these remarkable champions.

The Global Stage of Horse Racing

We begin by emphasizing the global stage on which horse racing unfolds. Racing transcends borders, with events held on every continent, attracting participants and spectators from diverse cultures and backgrounds.

The Significance of International Success

We discuss the importance of international success in horse racing. Winning on the global stage is a testament to a horse's exceptional talent and the skills of its connections, highlighting their ability to compete and excel beyond their home turf.

The Legacy of International Icons

The enduring legacy of international icons is celebrated. These horses have left a lasting mark on the sport, inspiring future generations and uniting racing enthusiasts worldwide in their shared admiration for the champions.

The Global Racing Community

We explore the worldwide racing community, a diverse and passionate group of individuals brought together by their love for the sport. This community spans the globe, from renowned racing hubs to emerging racing nations.

International Collaboration and Exchange

The role of international collaboration and exchange in the racing community is discussed. Connections between different countries have led to the sharing of knowledge, expertise, and the creation of a global racing network.

The Appeal of Iconic White and Grey Horses

We reflect on the unique appeal of white and grey coat colors in horse racing. These horses stand out as symbols of distinction and have captured the imaginations of fans worldwide.

Fan Engagement Beyond Borders

The global fan engagement with the featured horses is celebrated. Fans from different countries and backgrounds have come together to celebrate these champions, forming communities and fan clubs that bridge geographical divides.

International Racing Events

The impact of international racing events is explored. These events draw competitors from around the world and have become showcases of international talent, fostering a sense of camaraderie among racing communities.

Influence on Breeding Trends

We discuss how the bloodlines of iconic horses have influenced breeding trends. Their genetics continue to shape the future of racing, producing horses with the potential to achieve international acclaim.

The Global Racing Legacy

The worldwide racing community's connection to international success serves as a testament to the global appeal and enduring fascination of horse racing. The shared love for the sport and the remarkable champions featured in 'Whispers of Mist and Triumph' unite racing enthusiasts across the world.

The Universal Allure of Horse Racing

In closing, we emphasize the universal allure of horse racing, a sport that transcends borders and captures the hearts of individuals from all walks of life. The stories of these iconic racehorses are a testament to the power of racing to inspire, educate, and captivate the hearts of the worldwide racing community.

A Legacy that Knows No Borders

As we conclude our journey through the captivating stories of these equine heroes, we recognize that their legacies know no borders. The international success of these iconic racehorses and their profound influence on the worldwide racing community reinforce the notion that horse racing is a global endeavor, and the admiration for these champions is a shared passion that unites fans and enthusiasts from every corner of the globe.

A Tribute to Global Legends of the Turf

In this concluding section, we pay homage to the global legends of the turf featured in 'Whispers of Mist and Triumph.' These iconic white and grey racehorses have left an indelible mark on the world of horse racing and have become enduring symbols of excellence and inspiration.

The Remarkable Feats of Champions

We begin by reflecting on the remarkable feats of the featured champions. Their victories on the global stage, whether on different continents or in prestigious races, are celebrated as defining moments in racing history.

A Legacy of Excellence

The enduring legacy of these horses is highlighted. Their stories continue to inspire and educate, shaping the aspirations of future generations and serving as a reminder of the exceptional talent that graced the racing world.

International Success and Universal Appeal

We discuss the theme of international success and the universal appeal of these horses. Their ability to captivate the hearts of racing enthusiasts from diverse backgrounds underscores the global nature of the sport.

Influence on Breeding and Bloodlines

The impact of these iconic horses on the breeding industry is explored. Their genetics continue to shape the future of racing, producing horses with the potential to achieve international acclaim.

The Evolution of International Racing Events

We delve into the influence of these horses on the development of international racing events. Their participation in and victories at prestigious races have elevated these events to global spectacles, drawing competitors and spectators from around the world.

The Global Fanbase

We celebrate the worldwide fanbase that has formed around these champions. Racing enthusiasts from different countries and cultures have come together to support and share their passion for these remarkable horses.

International Recognition and Awards

The international recognition and awards received by these horses are discussed. Their rankings in prestigious awards, such as the Longines World's Best Racehorse Award, highlight their global acclaim.

Influence on Art and Culture

We reflect on how the stories of these iconic racehorses have influenced art, literature, and culture. Their narratives have inspired creative works that continue to honor their legacies and introduce their stories to new audiences.

Inspiration for Future Generations

The role of these horses as inspirations for future generations of racing enthusiasts is celebrated. Their stories serve as a source of motivation for young jockeys, trainers, breeders, and fans looking to make their mark in the racing world.

A Timeless Tribute

As we conclude our journey through the extraordinary stories of these equine heroes, we recognize that 'Whispers of Mist and Triumph' stands as a timeless tribute to global legends of the turf. The book's purpose is not only to celebrate their achievements but to preserve their legacies for future generations, ensuring that the remarkable feats of these iconic racehorses continue to captivate the hearts and minds of racing enthusiasts around the world.

THE END

Wordbook

Welcome to the glossary section of this book. Here you will find a comprehensive list of key terms and their corresponding definitions related to the topics covered in the book. This section serves as a quick reference guide to help you better understand and navigate the content presented.

1. Iconic Racehorses: Racehorses that have achieved remarkable success and are widely recognized and celebrated for their accomplishments.

2. White and Grey Coats: Refers to the coat colors of specific horses, often characterized by a lack of pigmentation, making them stand out in the racing world.

3. Global Feats: The extraordinary achievements of these horses on an international scale, including victories in prestigious races and competitions.

4. International Triumphs: Success and victories achieved by these racehorses in races and events held in various countries, signifying their global appeal.

5. World of Horse Racing: The entirety of the horse racing industry, including the races, events, participants, and enthusiasts involved in the sport.

6. Jockeys: The riders who guide and control the racehorses during races, playing a crucial role in their success.

7. Legacy: The lasting impact and influence that these iconic racehorses have had on the world of horse racing, even after their racing careers have ended.

8. Global Recognition: The widespread acknowledgment and admiration these horses have received from racing communities and fans worldwide.

9. Enduring Impact: The ongoing influence and significance of these racehorses in the history and development of horse racing.

10. Champions: A title given to horses that have achieved the highest level of success in their respective categories and races.

11. Cox Plate: A prestigious horse race held in Australia, notably won by some of the featured horses in the book.

12. Prix de l'Arc de Triomphe: A famous French horse race, showcasing the excellence of some of the horses discussed in the book.

13. Breeders' Cup Classic: An important American horse racing event, where some of the racehorses achieved significant victories.

14. Epsom Derby: A renowned British horse race, marking a milestone in the careers of certain featured horses.

15. Bloodlines: The lineage of a horse, including its parentage and ancestry, which can influence a horse's racing abilities.

16. Longines World's Best Racehorse Award: A prestigious accolade presented to the highest-performing racehorses globally.

17. Fan Engagement: The active involvement, support, and enthusiasm of racing fans for the featured horses and the sport.

18. Breeding Trends: The shifts and developments in horse breeding practices influenced by the genetics and success of these iconic racehorses.

Supplementary Materials

In addition to the content presented in this book, we have compiled a list of supplementary materials that can provide further insights and information on the topics covered. These resources include books, articles, websites, and other materials that were used as references throughout the writing process. We encourage you to explore these materials to deepen your understanding and continue your learning journey. Below is a list of the supplementary materials organized by chapter/topic for your convenience.

Introduction

Bowen, Edward L. "Masters of the Turf: Ten Trainers Who Dominated Horse Racing's Golden Age." University Press of Kentucky, 2007.

Chapter 1: Winx (Australia, 2011-2019), Bay (appeared greyish in some light)

"Winx: The Official Website." Accessed from [winxhorse.com.au](https://www.winxhorse.com.au/).

Chapter 2: Dancing Brave (United Kingdom, 1983-1999), Grey

Tanner, James. "Dancing Brave." J. A. Allen, 1986.

"Dancing Brave (horse)." Wikipedia. Accessed from https://en.wikipedia.org/wiki/Dancing_Brave_(horse).

Chapter 3: Zenyatta (United States, 2004-2020), Bay (appeared greyish in some light)

Moss, Jerry, and John Perrin. "Zenyatta: Queen of Racing." Daily Racing Form Press, 2011.

"Zenyatta (horse)." Wikipedia. Accessed from https://en.wikipedia.org/wiki/Zenyatta_(horse).

Chapter 4: Nashwan (United Kingdom, 1986-2002), Grey

Lynam, Ruth, and Robert Thornton. "Nashwan: A Celebration." Highdown, 2001.

"Nashwan (horse)." Wikipedia. Accessed from https://en.wikipedia.org/wiki/Nashwan_(horse).

Chapter 5: Global Triumphs Unveiled

Robertson, William H. "The History of Thoroughbred Racing in America." Henry Holt and Company, 1964.

Binns, Ronald C. "The International Thoroughbred." The Boydell Press, 2002.

Chapter 6: The World's Jockeys: Partners in Glory

Jones, Ron. "The Jockey's Guild." University Press of Kentucky, 2009.

"Jockey (horse racing)." Wikipedia. Accessed from https://en.wikipedia.org/wiki/Jockey_(horse_racing).

Chapter 7: A Global Legacy Beyond Borders

Balmer, Jeffrey, and Michael Johnson. "International Sport: A Bibliography, 1995-1999." Routledge, 2005.

"Legacy (horse)." Wikipedia. Accessed from https://en.wikipedia.org/wiki/Legacy_(horse).

Conclusion

Cook, Theodore Andrea. "The Turf." Longmans, Green, and Co., 1891.

"Horse Racing." Encyclopedia Britannica. Accessed from https://www.britannica.com/sports/horse-racing-sport.

www.ingramcontent.com/pod-product-compliance
Lightning Source LLC
LaVergne TN
LVHW012113070526
838202LV00056B/5709